Mortal Distractions

Mortal Distractions

PAULINE HOLDSTOCK

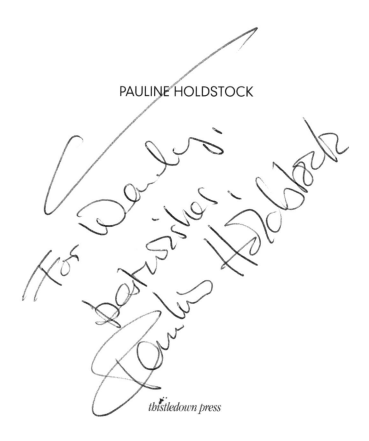

For Wendy,
best wishes,
Pauline Holdstock

thistledown press

Library and Archives Canada Cataloguing in Publication

Holdstock, Pauline, 1948-
        Mortal distractions / Pauline Holdstock.

Essays.
ISBN 1-894345-66-5

        I. Title.

PS8565.O622A16 2004   C814'.54   C2004-904340-4

Cover and book design by J. Forrie
Typeset by Thistledown Press
Printed and bound in Canada on acid-free paper

Thistledown Press Ltd.
633 Main Street, Saskatoon, Saskatchewan, S7H 0J8
www.thistledown.sk.ca

Canada Council
for the Arts
Conseil des Arts
du Canada

Canadian
Heritage
Patrimoine
canadien

SASKATCHEWAN
ARTS BOARD

Thistledown Press gratefully acknowledges the financial assistance of the Canada Council for the Arts, the Saskatchewan Arts Board, and the Government of Canada through the Book Publishing Industry Development Program for its publishing program.

ACKNOWLEDGEMENTS

The author gratefully acknowledges the support of the Canada Council for the Arts. She is grateful to Queenswood House for providing space to work.

"Truth To Tell" first appeared on the website www.dooneyscafe.com. "Reading the World" first appeared in the anthology *Brothers, Borders and Babylon*, edited by M. Florczak (Jervis Distributors). "Ship of Fools" was first published in *Prairie Fire* and was the winner of the *Prairie Fire* Personal Journalism Prize in 2000. "Catch" has appeared on the website www.opendemocracy.net. A version of "Mine! Mine! Mine!" was published by the *National Post* under the title "That's My Idea". "Of Remnants and Riches" was first published in the anthology *Going Some Place*, edited by Lynne Van Luven (Coteau Books). A part of "Can ID" first appeared in *Geist* under the title "In This Country".

The author wishes to thank House of Anansi for permission to quote from the works of Anne Hébert. The author extends grateful thanks to Terrence Malick for permission to quote from his film *The Thin Red Line*.

Special thanks to Seán Virgo for his expert guidance.

Contents

For my family

and for my friends
old and new

with love

TRUTH TO TELL

I HAVE A STORY TO TELL. Whether it is a true story is a question for later. I must still negotiate the first sentence where "have" is something of a stumbling block but is, all the same, the word I want to use. I was not born with the story, nor did I take it. I neither wanted it nor asked for it. But it was told to me and now that I have it I am compelled by the story itself — by its unquiet nature and the questions it raises — to pass it on.

There is a man is working outside in a shed, splitting wood with his two sons. It is a rainy west coast night with no moon. A single light bulb hangs from a cord slung over a rafter. There is a chopping block under the light. While the older boy works with the axe, the father stacks the wood. The younger boy is picking up kindling.

The three of them work in the centre of the shed in the pool of light. There is not much room to move about and they are all getting tired but the younger boy is still eager. When he reaches forward to the block just as his brother's axe comes down, the blow severs two of his fingers.

The family acts quickly. The boy's mother binds his hand, wraps the fingers in a cloth and all of them drive as quickly as possible to the hospital ten minutes down the road.

9

When they arrive at the Emergency unit the nurse in Reception points to the chairs lined up opposite the desk. She asks for the father's name.

The father tells her it's an emergency, his son is hurt very badly. He tells her what has happened.

The nurse turns and calls a question back into the room behind her.

Someone answers and she turns back.

"The doctor for Indians is off duty, she says. "But he'll be on again at six."

The boy sits for the rest of the night in the waiting room, holding his fingers wrapped in a bundle on his lap.

That's it. No more details, no waiting room drama. The story as I've recounted it mirrors as nearly as I can recall the story that was told — in the first person — to members of a small advocacy group for Native justice. The details are spare. I can't even tell you the ages of the boys, though I can guess at seven and twelve. The teller — the man who as a boy lost two fingers — left us to sit with our own shock and our unanswered questions in much the same way that the nurse in the story left the family to sit with their pain.

If you are non-Native you are left with an overriding question. If you are Native you don't bother to ask because you know, have known for more than a hundred years. How could this happen? It is a question asked in disbelief — while still believing.

But if you care to take the question further, the answers that turn up are disconcerting. That it happened is not in any doubt at all. But when you ask "How?", it seems the story may not quite support all the inferences you've made.

What took place in the emergency room and the words that were spoken there, as they are remembered and recounted by members of the family's community, imply a quite specific situation:

— a family has come to seek emergency surgery to sew back on the severed fingers of a young boy

— the boy is forced to wait all night for treatment

— the chance to reattach the fingers is lost.

But the questions prompted by the story lead incidentally to aspects that subtly alter the violence of its colouring. Firstly, in the 1960s, when the event took place, reanastomosis — the surgical procedure involved in reattaching severed members — was not a technique known or practiced in the emergency rooms of Canadian hospitals. It became a viable option only during the 1970s. It is doubtful whether it would have occured to medical practioners in an emergency unit at the time of the story. (Although I've no doubt at all that it might occur in the minds of any, of all, parents in the same situation, regardless of the current state of technology or their own knowledge of it.)

Secondly, at that period there would have been no specially trained emergency room physician of any kind on duty. There would have been an intern to give interim care while the patient's own doctor, in this case 'the doctor for the Indians', was called. Putting the two facts together, you can see at once how the outrage at the heart of the story is diluted. (Though other questions whose answers are not contained within the story remain. Did the intern administer any care? Was the doctor not called before morning and why not? etc.)

All of which poses something of a problem, for I do want to believe. It is a powerful story and I want to tell it. Already I can think of three or four people who would do well to listen to it. It is the story to demolish all ifs and buts about the need for restitution and justice. Not only that, its metaphorical heft is impressive — and that's hard for a writer to resist.

But the new light I myself have just cast on the story is a problem. If I repeat it now as I heard it, I will find myself in the position of being able to offend my artistic and my moral integrity at the same time. I shall betray my personal belief — that only the truth (the whole truth etc., etc.) has the power to restore and redeem, or at the very least that without the truth no healing can begin. Still, my dented scruples are a minor hurt set against the injury I might otherwise inflict on those connected with the story, for to tell it now in any other way would be to rewrite someone else's reality. To call any detail into question is to heap more injury on the man with two fingers missing, who transgressed his own cultural constraints (of privacy, of propriety etc) to repeat his story outside his own community, who is, and knows himself to be, a living metaphor for the dismemberment of his people.

The reality for the boy, the man, and by extension (because he himself has taken on the character of symbol) his people, is that the *experience* of inhumanity is central to his life. Whether it was a direct result of that night or a consequence of everything that went before and continues to come after hardly matters any more. Analysis is not the right response. All those in the community who repeat the story are speaking wholly and only what they deem to be the truth.

The way out of this impasse must be to listen to what is being said, to listen and to really hear. The only way to respond to this story is in the same spirit in which it is told. Truth will not necessarily (will rarely?) present itself in neat analytic packages. It may come in forms that we do not readily recognize, especially when our minds are trained by the printed word. Within the community where this event took place, the tradition of story telling is still alive. No discourse or debate takes place without the inclusion of quite lengthy factual or even fictional oral accounts; these are not illustrations of a truth but *are* the receptacles of it. To listen to this story in the spirit of this kind of truth-telling is to begin to have your heart and mind opened to someone else's experience — and to another means of establishing the truth.

It opens, too, the question of the relevance of authenticity and reveals how the truth, the validity of an experience, may be carried intact in the leaky vessel of fiction. Good non-fiction writing and good fiction are equally capable of presenting the social and political conventions of our time — and then reaching beyond them. As a writer I could add details of my own to the story, could make the lamp swing and the power dip when a tree touches the line outside, could make the father turn, his arms full of wood, to see the two brothers staring at the block, could show the fingers like salamanders frozen in the light. I could make the cloth to wrap them checkered, could have an uncle drive the car, could make him park all askew in his haste to get into Emergency. The story as I have told it may already, technically, *be* fiction. *Was* it the mother who wrapped the fingers? Was it the father or was it an uncle who was working with the brothers? I can't say. Was the younger boy eager to help? Is my version less true? More?

And what about the role of the listeners in all this? The narrator's instincts were one hundred percent accurate — or true — in the telling of his story. He knew exactly what he was doing when he left us, his listeners, that day, with the image of the boy in the waiting room. For don't we all want to fill in the blanks? And once we've painted in our own details — the mother cradling the boy, the father pacing the floor — is it still a true story we carry away with us? Truth has always been absolute . . . *hasn't* it? Questions can only mean one hasn't arrived yet at the thing that is true, the place where no questions arise.

The reality at the heart of the story is pain. The validity of the experience of the pain lies within the confines of the story itself, not in facts to be authenticated outside it. The story is a dramatic indictment of our social and political history and its consequences, yet it wields its power not because of any attention to details of recent history but because of the deeper truth it reveals about the capacity of men and women to turn their backs on each other.

This should be the place where there are no more questions. Yet still there is something unsatisfactory. To distill this story down to the generality of man's inhumanity to man would be to deny, or at least to gloss over, the specific oppression of one group of people by another. Men and women with power are more prone to inflict injury than to suffer it; yes, we all have the capacity to turn our backs, to inflict pain, but that these things can be done *only* from a position of power nevertheless remains the most uncomfortable truth of all, in itself the single most pressing argument for an urgent redistribution of power and resources — and responsibility. We can reject the burden of guilt for the sins and blunderings of someone else's fathers — but not the responsibility to make restitution. Present political reality will always be the product of history; that's always been the easy get-out for those who don't want to change it. But history is not over and done with; it's the river we swim in, as ongoing as the present moment; and tomorrow's political world is already being shaped by what we do, or don't do, today.

So there is the story. Because finally, isn't it an artist's duty, her only duty, to tell the truth? And the truth of the matter is that once, not so long ago, a small boy sat all night waiting for the doctor for the Indians.

READING THE WORLD

IN THE LOUNGE AT HEATHROW AIRPORT a little after three o'clock on the afternoon of September 11th, a group of men in suits have drawn their chairs up in a tight horseshoe in front of the TV. I walk past, incurious. In these lounges there are always men in suits glued to the TV. It is their world — sports, stocks, wars. They are always watching it.

Over at the cappuccino machine fragments of commentary from the TV begin to penetrate — "hit", "plane", "live", "New York". There is an uncanny atmosphere in the room. I turn back toward the viewers, seeing their faces now for the first time, each man in the crowd utterly isolated in his connection to the screen where it is morning in New York and something inexplicable is happening. No one is saying anything. The only sound in the room is the live broadcast spilling from the TV. A white-coated steward is tidying the coffee station.

The cold-bloodedness of the attack poleaxes the brain. The terrible simplicity of this new way of dealing death. And the stupidity. Poking a bear in the eye.

"And now — a death machine, là! Là! Just beneath my window! Have I engendered it? It seems that I have." These are the words of de Sade (in Rikki Ducornet's novel, *The Fanmaker's Inquisition*) as he watches the newly-invented guillotine in bloody action in the square just outside his prison window: the hitherto unimagined (by him) and therefore unimaginable has joined with the imagined (by some other) to create its own cataclysmic reality. The world of the possible made horribly one with the world of the real. Nothing is unimaginable. And nothing that can be imagined is impossible. And what were the thoughts, on the morning of September 11th, of all those who deal in, perpetrate, perpetuate, uphold, and excuse violence? What were the weapons inventors, the arms dealers thinking as they watched the news unfold? What were the creators of stealth bombers and biochemical weapons and smart bombs and cruise missiles saying? Did they, like the fictional de Sade, whisper in their shock, "I am outdone!" As he says, "It is one thing to dream of massacres; it is another to witness one."

It's time to board; I'm travelling to Nice with my husband. In the concourse outside the lounge, we pass through milling crowds who have not yet heard the news. I'm wondering if perhaps even the flight attendants taking our boarding passes have not heard. What else can we do but get on? We want to get out of Heathrow. We can't fly back to our children in Canada. We go about the business of boarding with this new and ugly lump of information lodged in the brain, unprocessed. Everything is askew. This is the disjunction that will infect consciousness throughout the globe and create the myth of a changed world.

The freight of new information stowed in our conscious-ness gives an otherwise routine and uneventful flight an air of freakish unreality. We are in a comfortable, upholstered limbo — or perhaps a bomb. We should be going home.

17

Though we don't know it yet, we are on the last plane to fly in to Nice for the next five days.

Cannes, our destination, is a town covered by the tracks and spores of exorbitant personal wealth. Here even the pink sand beach, with its high mica content, glitters. All the planes are grounded and will remain so for the duration of our stay. In the hotel room we watch the shining towers come down, and come down, and come down . . . How the mind refuses the two dimensional. It is like a macabre magic trick. Show me again. The following day, sitting out away from the town and the beach, I spread out *Cannes-Matin* on a rock. "L'Apocalypse" in letters four inches high. The clarity of these photographs. The glass towers. The black shapes of the tiny human stars falling against the blue.

Friday, the day of mourning. Visitors here, we are without community. At 11 o'clock white-coated waiters from the luxury hotel across the street assemble to stand in silence beside the swimming pool. Some car horns sound. Most people go about their business.

My children are eight thousand kilometres away.

I've brought J.M. Coetzee's *Disgrace* away with me, a perverse choice of holiday reading but its themes now strangely appropriate: death as the ultimate disgrace; the profound shame implicit in violence; the dehumanizing power of destruction. And now this new means of destruction. How are we to live with our common humanity, double-edged sword that it is? I am disgusted to be part of the human race. In another of Coetzee's books, *Lives of the Animals*, his protagonist rejects the sum of the philosophical achievements of rational humanity and places herself squarely on the side of the unknowing animals. It's where I want to be.

There is an American flag flying outside one of the hotels at the forlorn western extremity of the *plage du Midi*. It's faded almost beyond recognition, worn almost to transparency by the wind. A long shred of fabric waves out in a helpless, hopeless fashion against the sky's brilliant blue. From a certain angle, when you look up at the flag you see a single, skinny palm towering behind it, impossibly tall, its fronds flipped up and over in a cocky crest. Hollywood could not match the pedantry of this symbolism.

September 16th. The airports are open. We fly home today. Our place in the line through the many security checks is behind an Arab couple. We are excessively friendly towards them, trying to convey by our manner that we would not for a moment consider them in any way implicated, trying to alleviate any shame they might be feeling in what is becoming known as the "terrible events". They for their part respond with equally exaggerated warmth. No amount of security checking could be too much. He jokes that the only answer is to have all passengers disrobe at a check point and board the plane in hospital gowns. This is funny. But instead of hospital gowns I keep thinking body bags. Three months later a passenger on an American Airlines jet will try to ignite the explosives he has hidden in his shoes.

Heathrow airport is choc-a-bloc. A fellow in our line asks strangers behind him to mind his bag. He is going to look for a doughnut. I summon one of the many policemen to the scene. As if he could save any of us, least of all our distant families, should bag become bomb. My action provokes a marital dispute of high comedy that lasts almost until we board the plane. For the duration of the ten-hour flight my husband reads the *Observer*, the *Sunday Times* and the *Independent* in their entirety. I pray to Saint Christopher and read a little 45-page book on compost. I read it over and over.

Gardening Without Digging was first published in Britain in 1947 by an amateur Yorkshire gardener, A. Guest. The green and black art work on the cover of my copy, a reissue of the 1949 edition, shows a contented family man (we know this by his pipe) leaning against a tree in full suit and tie as he surveys row upon row of burgeoning cabbages. During the Second World War Britons were encouraged by the Government to grow 'victory gardens', supplementing scarce food supplies with their own produce The habit continued through the years of food rationing. The emphasis was on productivity but an additional benefit must have been the consolation of the earth, its constancy when homes, loved ones could disappear overnight. The booklet is nicely printed on glossy stock and contains grainy photographs of the author's successes: *Here Mr. Guest is dwarfed by his runner beans and eleven peas in a pod are common.* He was a man ahead of his time and I fall for him at the opening words, "Applying compost on top of undug soil is simply a copy of nature's methods which have been tested and proved by nature for centuries." His photograph shows him standing up to his armpits in winter wheat "sown without ploughing, in October 1948." His set mouth and steady gaze are speaking to me: *You can't deny this.* I'm soothed even by the section headings: *Fight or Cooperate? . . . Nature Reveals her Secret . . . More Tributes to*

Compost. In some of the photographs, a folding ruler, like the one my father used, is set down beside the vegetables. I can't get enough of the solidity of these onions, these leeks and parsnips. I could almost pray to their creator, the pseudonymous Mr. Guest. My children are eight thousand kilometres away.

September 18th. Safely back in Canada, reunited with my family, I can stop holding my breath, holding the planes aloft. Relieved of my duty of controlling the skies, I begin to read voraciously, all those British Sundays, the *Globe and Mail*, the *National Post*. They help and they don't help. Opinion, projection, analysis: these are the tools we are accustomed to use for political situations. They inform us but they also detach, taking us further from the unmediated apprehension of the event. Robert Fisk is good. So is John Le Carré. I read forwarded emails, texts of other writers, Tamim Ansary the Afghan-American, Slavoj Zizek's essay, "The Desert of the Real", found on the internet. But it's the words of Robin Morgan in another email forwarded from New York that reach the heart:
"Who could have imagined it: the birds were burning."

The media eventually outrun their usefulness. Journalists who rose to the occasion with informed commentary and tight writing are beginning to treat themselves to self-indulgent posturing. Everywhere rhetoric replaces content as America prepares to retaliate. And something else is happening. Now there is yet another celebrity benefit, now another televised memorial. Debord was right. We are reducing all life, all living, to spectacle. With jaw-dropping absence of irony, someone — Bette Midler? Barbara

Streisand? — is singing "Wind Beneath My Wings". On one of the networks a show is built around September 11th: "Heroes at Ground Zero". People are searching for a way to keep that surge of love for humanity alive. It is a kind of emotional masturbation, trying to keep it going after the moment. But it's not possible. The only way to rekindle it is to commit an act of compassion. It's why people send money. It's why bombing should be inconceivable.

There is much more that is unhelpful, and all of it taking us further from ground zero. With rhetoric and bombast, with interminable analysis and self-censorship we are screening ourselves from the blinding perception of the moment which in itself contained all that was useful in dealing with it. Soon we will be reduced to discussing the legality of the Government's acquisition of antibiotics against chemical attack, the implications of a country dropping crackers and peanut butter on the same people it is bombing, and (this will appear on a Netscape daily poll) what scares us most ("anthrax, suicide bomber, hijacker, or nuclear bomb").

The moment is going. I know in my heart, it's already gone.

And so what was it in that moment that we needed at all costs to salvage? In that split second, no one had been demonized, the word evil hadn't been mentioned and al-Quaeda wasn't even in our lexicon. We looked terror in the eye and it revealed itself. What we saw was the *human* heart and mind in deadly concert. That was what made it such a monstrous perversion of human potential — but no aberration. What we experienced was the deepest disgrace of the human condition. And that's what we needed to hold in our own minds and hearts to save ourselves from its obscenity. Bombing too is a human act.

In every catastrophe there is an instant when terror ignites compassion. It's when you weep for Bolivian farmers buried in a mud slide, for the massacre of a kindergarten class in Scotland. It's when the relatives of the victims in New York could say, as the mother of one fireman said: "Let there be no more hatred. Let no more blood be shed." Compassion is fired by the particular but its purview is limitless. For a few hours, perhaps a few days, change seems a real possibility. What if the US could be pressured into reacting *without* violence? But "What if?" is quickly fading to "as if" and the president is amassing international support for a war.

I search out an unread copy of the Qur'an. It remains unread. I keep opening it at random and I keep finding a God dressed just like the God of the Old Testament, a God for times of tribal warfare. To serve him now is to serve the appetite of the tribe.

In my despair as a pacifist trying to come to terms with the need for action in the defence of the most basic moral precepts, I turn to a writer from the first half of the twentieth-century, one with strong connections to New York. An early aviator, Antoine de Saint-Exupéry regularly risked his life in flimsy and unreliable machines in order to deliver the mails, often at night, to remote regions. Flying was his joy and his passion. Most of his writing is a celebration of the marvellous union of man and machine and the elements. The act of flying, for him, was made possible by the brilliance of human creativity and by the courage of the pilots and navigators. Equipment on these early planes was rudimentary. Flight could only be sustained by careful attention to the wind and the stars and to the lovely and dangerous contours of the earth. His own solitary voyages between the earth and the stars gave Saint-Exupéry a steep perspective on the world and time to contemplate. Respect for mankind, our only way forward, he said, is in deepest peril when it is most urgently needed.

For a few weeks Saint-Exupéry is all I can read. He is the very antithesis of the hijackers. His writings, infused with wonder at the consistently surprising beauty of the planet and with respect for its awesome powers, are a testament to his sense of common humanity, his sense of comradeship with all those who labour in the service of others; he places the airman alongside the postman, the miner, the ploughman, the fisherman. I am glad he died before men loaded planes with nuclear bombs and released them on cities, before men flew passenger planes into hundred-storey buildings.

When war broke out in 1939, Saint Exupéry wrestled with the dilemma that conflict brings: to "save" peace is to know the disgrace of inaction in the face of others' pain; to sacrifice peace is to discover the deep shame of war. In the end Saint-Exupéry chose active service and flew with a French squadron as a reconnaissance pilot. Later, when France fell, he served with an American squadron. But he refused to fly bombers.

The Afghan people are pouring out of their own country. To counteract the talk of air strikes and military targets and Taliban strongholds, I put up a photograph on the fridge of an Afghan boy of about seven carrying his baby sister on his back. I know that among the refugees there must be men who have betrayed their own humanity for the sake of a political cause or a religious belief, perhaps for a simple bribe — just as I know that in those burning towers, besides the cleaners and the firemen and the receptionists, there must have been men and women who daily betrayed their own conscience, increasing the world's burden of hardship and pain for the sake of an economic ideal, the promise of global trade, their own definition of "progress", or simply for profit. But I will not shut down the heart.

Now on TV the images are all of the war. Several stark-eyed, bearded prisoners are seated on the ground. They must be Taliban or we wouldn't be seeing this. Guards with rifles stand by. A duckling waddles in from the right of the picture, unnoticed by the prisoners who continue to watch their guards apprehensively. The prisoners' faces are haggard. So are the guards'. You can't help but wonder what happens after these pictures are taken. The duckling waddles and stops a few feet in front of them. It turns its head to preen the feathers of its back before it walks on.

SHIP OF FOOLS

STANDING AT THE RAIL, I'm watching the last shreds of glamour drop away into the vertiginous gap between ship and quay. And we have not even cast off. It had already been trampled in the scrimmage of the embarkation hall. The belligerent US immigration officer finished it off. I can see him there still at the foot of the gangway. Like a mediaeval reminder of hell for the poor fools who think they are on their way to paradise, his was the last face we saw on land.

That illusion, anyway, was never safe with me. I've always had trouble joining the party, and this is a party, pure froth, a rare indulgence. I'm on a mini-cruise to Alaska paid for by my (poor-old-widowed?) mother from England. She calls it the trip of her lifetime and she had no difficulty persuading me to leave my principles and my teenagers at home and accompany her — I was more than ready to lie back and think of Canada. As we prepare to sail, however, I cannot suppress the thought that we are a ship of fools. My eyes now will be stuck open and I shall be fated once again to play the blind seer, the prophet of doom, the bloody-minded passenger in 524 who is being difficult. The ugly-tempered guardian at the gate has put me on the wrong foot and I fear I shall never be in step.

The expensive backdrop of Canada Place, a look-alike, land-locked cruise-ship of a building begins to recede and a speck of a tug coaxes us into mid-channel. There is a spattering of cheers and applause. The waiters come by again for orders from the bar. I am painfully aware that this is a high-tech, high-consumption vessel with enormous potential for pollution and the spread of disease (in many more ways than one) — nothing less in fact than the perfect metaphor for our planet, we ourselves the restless, aimless, greedy, self-indulgent souls upon her. But there are no hair-shirts in the dress code.

It's a temptation to be taking notes, yet no one likes to feel that there's a guest at the party intent on souring the punch, and the stance of critical observer is not one that endears you to your fellow revellers (or, for that matter, your mother). It's uncomfortably close to where the misanthrope stands — it's almost in her shoes. But we are underway and it's time to get acquainted with this floating planet.

Others are doing the same. An exasperated (already after only thirty minutes? Thirty years?) fellow with a Brooklyn accent is telling his wife to listen. "Da gambling is at da front, da food is at da back. It's all you gotta remember, OK?" Her reply shows a fine sense of our common predicament, "So where are we, then?"

The way to survive a mass experience must be always to go against the grain, to swim upstream, be in the wrong place at the right time. This suits my mother who in the course of her life has learned the clever trick of both charting her own course and at the same time taking in many a colourful regatta along the way. We spend the afternoon up on deck drinking the air and having our souls raked by the cries of seagulls. The sun deck is for me where this cruise will happen, sun or rain. Here there is no piped music, there is no false front — which would only be ripped away by the weather — no glitter, and there is nothing for sale. There is only the long, varnished rail, damp in the mist, the scrubbed-to-whiteness deck, and the wind. The stewards give us thick red and black chequered blankets to wrap ourselves against the damp, removing the spent mugs of tea as discretely as if they were empty whisky bottles. The hours slip by like water. Life is effortless, effort-free . . . We are pleasantly anaesthetised; there is no weight attached to our choice of destination for we shall return; there is no time constraint, for we'll not mind a delay. For us there is no responsibility, no duty. Good-bye Kant. Our moral lives are in suspension, our physical lives provided for; there is nothing to attend to and so (here is the clever trick) we can at last attend. We can attend to the view, to the water, to the mountains gliding ghostly in the mist; we can attend to ourselves. We can pay attention to the majesty of the planet, or to the taste of salt on the lip. We might even pay attention to the voice within.

Buddhism here of all places. But I am not really surprised. Transient, I am most centred; I become who I am. Cut off from the disruptions of friends and family and the interruptions of work, everything calms down. There is time to catch a breath. Contemplation becomes fruitful. Ideas flow, free of hidden agendas, true to themselves and not twisted into shapes that don't become them.

It is time to go below and dress for dinner. Next, a leisurely stroll through the ship. I would find it all faintly embarrassing were it not for a fortifying cocktail. Is everyone feeling this way? I don't think so. Many look utterly serious about this business of swanning around like plutocrats. I do an excellent job at disguising my disaffection and my mother does an excellent job at restraining her enthusiasm. We meet in genuine astonishment at this boat's over-the-top opulence. Look, we could be in a James Bond film. My mother — who is eighty-two — languishes beside a fountain that appears to rain gold from a sea-fan. She could be twenty, thirty years younger. There is something to be said for taking life as you find it, diving in.

When we reach the dining room, however, engagement seems less desirable. Seven hundred and fifty souls are leaving in dribs and drabs. Seven hundred and forty-eight are waiting for the second sitting. Seven hundred and fifty counting ourselves. It is a crazy planet we are on — or rather, we are crazies on this planet, spinning through time and space, riding our mad pleasure machine.

When we are all finally seated at our tables of eight, our dinner companions take our measure and we theirs. We are all polite and tamely jocose. Among us is a pleasant Canadian couple celebrating forty years of marriage. Both are amiable and full of goodwill, at ease with each other and with the world; the husband, a stone mason of Sicilian extraction, is outgoing with a natural charm and a fine sense of humour. He's not a man to be taken in by affectation, a man who even in a dinner jacket would order fish and chips if he wanted them. He tells us about the best place to go for halibut in Ketchikan where we will spend a day. He likes my mother, recognizes her as one of his own kind.

Not surprisingly, dinner is lavish, epicurean. I see the moral dilemma that rears its head as soon as one begins to poke about in the world: how to live in a consumer society without doing harm, that is, without becoming an agent of injury to the planet and to ourselves and others.

Thinking even for a minute about the quantities of food consumed and wasted here on this ship, the chemicals involved in its production, the fuel burned in its transportation, is enough to give me indigestion. Obviously one cannot sit at the overladen table *and* preach justice. But either you are in the world or out of it, and if you are in it you qualify for automatic implication. How then to agitate for change? I spend much of my time as a writer teasing at these questions. Naively, I did not expect to come away with them. I do not want to be Savonarola. I keep tossing the hair shirt overboard. It keeps reappearing in my luggage.

We take a walk on the deserted promenade deck after dinner. There might be some parallel wistful souls on the starboard side of the universe but everyone else is inside in the bars, or at the casino, or taking their seats for the magic show. The magic show. Out here the water is very black and the ship's lights are stars appearing and disappearing as it folds on itself. Vanishing.

❖

Breakfast is a feast. We are awash with the juice of fresh, ripe fruit, stuffed with treats, sweet and savoury. The coffee is good and never runs out. I finally taste the illusion. Hoary old conscience hobbles by the door, noticing the heaps of food being carted away on the dirty plates. I turn my back on her and step outside to watch the mountains, which have spent the night slipping closer and growing taller, gently tearing the morning mist. This is heaven.

There is this morning, up here on the sun deck, a select gathering of the self-righteous. We exchange covert glances of hoarded joy, secret pleasure in the magnificence of the setting and in our own moral and physical hardiness, for the weather remains cool and damp and there are, we know, people inside who are queuing for bingo tickets and checking the time of the indoor golf tournament in the midship bar, where plastic fir trees have been set up on the carpet.

Later when I go down I see a huge crowd gathered on one of the atrium decks. A poster announces a sale of 'Fine Jewellery'. Passengers are jostling for the chance to "shop with confidence and save fifty percent." I want to see what it is we cannot be expected to live without, what might keep us from the soft mists and the salt spray. There is a selection of chains, links, ropes and clasps in gold, things that bind, things that pierce and hold, miniature fetters for Marley's ghost. There are flowers and leaves and birds caught, all, in gold. I remember earlier someone outside on deck asking where we were and the reply: Desolation Sound.

There is a forward lounge on this boat, high above the water and domed entirely in glass for a panoramic view. It is the casino. The machines operate from seven in the evening. During the day it is deserted except for the free lessons in gaming and slots at ten. The lessons are part of the activities program which includes scarf-tying, art appreciation, and the anti-cellulite inch loss seminar. The daily bulletin can be depressing. It does not do to comb it too closely. Better to go back on deck and play at being Edwardians again.

I try to sort out what this ship is really about while my mother reads or chats with other passengers. I'm in deep dismay at what I see in parts of this ship and yet I should not be, or at least I should not be surprised. The desensitisation to the natural world, the materialism, the gluttony, the consumerism — we've displayed a natural talent for all of these on land.

Did I expect it to be any different? Travelling, we are still ourselves. Look at me with my notebook and my inability to connect; Emily, my mother, with her gregarious optimism. I have chosen a deck chair away from anyone else: Emily has been quietly attracting company all afternoon, passing strangers who willingly, eagerly even, divulge intimate details of their lives to her and with whom she unfailingly finds a common bond. Often it will have to do with places in our own lives ten thousand miles and twenty years away. "Can you believe it! The lady in the blue comes from Billericay? Amazing isn't it? And you see that man by the stairs, well his son apparently . . . " Life is always amazing for Emily. She needs neither napkin-folding lessons in the Interludes Lounge nor a heli-trip to sight grizzly bears. She already has the only skill she needs. Perhaps the cruise line could manage a seminar on it: *The Art of Amazement: Find out how you can drop old habits of cynicism and replace them with new skills of wonder. Learn the art of fascination 11 AM in the Gull's Wing.* I'd attend.

A rare announcement from the bridge tells us that we are approaching Bella Bella. The port rail fills with passengers, craning for the first glimpse of the Heiltsuk community. Many have binoculars trained on the village. It does not look so different from the Native community close to where I live, only perhaps a little more prosperous. Low wooden houses, roads, cars and trucks, the odd satellite dish. We must look like an iced confection floating by. An extra-terrestrial wedding cake. It is certain that we momentarily obliterate the further bank of the channel from the view of those on shore. Are there still fish to be had in this stretch of water? I hope that some of the inhabitants have their own binoculars and are scrutinising us.

I know now what the ship is about. It is about keeping the customer not satisfied but hostage. It is a floating entertainment centre selling the illusion of experience (living) while keeping its customers, its consumers, insulated from it (life); it is doing what large corporations do to us all the time: ensuring that we remain in effect in the shopping mall. Our job is to purchase the fine cruise wear and souvenirs, feed the slots and above all consume the alcohol. We could of course venture into the backdrop, the scenery, but we have forgotten how; we should need to take an excursion, purchasing first a seat in the capsule of the train, the helicopter, purchasing the controlled, the packaged experience. This ship is about the planet we find ourselves on, the world we have allowed to happen.

❖

Day three. Six-thirty. I draw back the curtains. Our window is filled completely with the facade of a wooden, steel-roofed building on this quay where we have apparently docked in the night. *THREE FLOORS OF SHOPPING!* proclaims the banner that runs the entire breadth of the building. But who has time for more jaundiced observations? We are utterly caught up in the particular magic of sea travel. You go to bed while sliding on the surface of the water and you fall asleep, lulled by a kind of subliminal motion, very quickly, very easily. And you wake, six or seven hours later, in another part of the world, amazed (at last!) to find that, while you slept, loyal minions of the company were beavering away to reverse the engines, radio the shore, check the radar, the sonar, ask the pilot if his wife has had her kid, sling lines round mooring pins (so nineteenth century) and let down the gangway all for you. Now that's a thrill. I put another roll of film in the camera.

Nothing on the way up the thickly carpeted stairs prepares me for the shock of the view from the top deck. There is a cruise ship moored in front of us and one aft. Combined, we are bigger than the town. When I go to the stern and hold the camera vertically to take a shot of the next boat, the resulting picture is split in two. The town is on the right hand half, the ship on the left; the visual space they occupy is exactly equivalent. We are visitors from Brobdignag with the twist that we shall be Lilliputianised the instant our feet touch dry land. Down on the quay-side a tour group of tiny people (folk?) is already gathering in their red and yellow, their forest green and purple. The poor-old-widowed and I do not have the energy or the resources for a tour. We shall spend the day in the port. I like the idea of really seeing where it is we really have arrived.

While we are finding boots and coats and hats, we switch on our TV for the first time to see if it will give us a weather forecast. There on the screen is — live — the three floors of shopping that are outside the window. The window, I notice now, is a fat rectangle with rounded corners, the exact shape in fact of a TV screen. Emily and I ad lib a sketch that involves two alcoholic women watching the entire cruise from their berths.

Down in the town, the ships have each disgorged their fifteen hundred or so to the mercies of the purveyors of knick-knacks. We wander about with a dazed and vaguely demented air. The press of people must be seen to be believed. I stop to ask a woman wearing a brand new traditional red and black blanket and selling tours, how many times a week this number descends on her town. Oh, every day, she says cheerfully. Three boats every day? Oh no, she says. Seven, maybe more sometimes, and she nods towards the dock where one ship has already left and another is taking its place. There are three more standing off in the narrows. I can't begin to process this information and do not try. Emily and I, possibly the only two visitors of eight or nine thousand today (fifty, sixty thousand this week?), take a local bus which for one dollar makes a long leisurely loop around the port. The residents have a chance to stare back: *What, here as well, on my way to/from work/home?* What seemed like a good idea begins to feel suspiciously like an intrusion. We have jumped the rails, left the circuit. It is a kind of tourist faux pas. We should be spending dollars in the town. We are glad to get back, and merge with the crowd, though we leave it again at lunch-time in search of the fabled halibut. We find it in a tiny burger-hut of a place that has clearly evolved from a van. It has service from the counter and ketchup on the table and the halibut is, as our dinner companion promised, the finest we have tasted.

So there it is again, the behemoth of capitalism nosing into every bay and inlet. At least the fish hut operator appreciated our presence and we his. I think of a conversation I had with a Native writer, not on tourism but on the dispersal of Europeans across North America. I don't understand it, he said. What are all you people *doing* roaming around? Don't you have any families? I knew what he meant. It is strange behaviour to leave as I did, one's family, one's roots for no significant reason other than that one could. (Though were I a refugee from Sarajevo or Rwanda or Chile or Somalia, I should have felt affronted and hurt. No we don't all have families.) The sub-text I inferred was: Why don't you all stay home? Well yes. This is the feeling that touring gives me: What am I doing here? Why don't we all go home and leave these people alone? But what then? Are we all to live in isolated pockets and meet only to skirmish at our borders? There are no easy answers. Even eco-tourism is fraught with well-intentioned blunders. We are indeed a ship of fools.

It is late afternoon and the collective madness has infected us all. By the end of the day, in a terrible analogy for the way we squander our time on earth, we are reduced to glassy-eyed idiots dithering over whether fudge made in Milwaukee or coasters made in Taiwan would be more appreciated by our neighbours.

❖

This morning we sail under a blue, blue sky with the sunlight rebounding from every surface of the dazzling ship. I have zipped my notebook firmly into the back of my suitcase. We are going to play at being Barbie by the pool. All day. With everyone else. We are going to sip long drinks and I shall have a swim. And we do. And I do. And it is very good. A sad couple nearby is having not such a good time. They are in their late twenties. When he brings a plate of salad to his reclining chair, she says, Gee thanks. Look after yourself why don't you? He says, I thought you were asleep? She says, You know I wasn't. You kicked my foot when you left. He says, Why didn't you answer then? She says, Because

36

you kicked my foot, and they carry on for quite a while, the thrill all gone. The group to our right is more cheerful. They are in their mid thirties, have given up for a while on thrills and settled for getting along. There are three men and three women and they are enjoying each other, each in her, his, assigned role. They spend a lot of time laughing at private jokes and shared memories and they slip from time to time into improvised comedy routines. They are in a familiar easy groove and they are happy. These are people to take on a holiday.

Tonight at dinner there is an additional warmth to our exchanges. We are all old hands, relaxed and convivial. We have all survived each other, nor have we been punished in any way for the outrageous hubris of taking to sea in this giant floating meringue. Only two of the party are quieter, more thoughtful than before and it is neither my mother nor I but the middle-aged couple who did not go ashore in port yesterday choosing instead to spend all day on board. I surmise that it is a new, late-blooming relationship and that they too have discovered that they are who they are. They are either appalled at what they have learned or pining to return to the new world within their cabin.

The other married couple at the table is more genial than ever. One of the company buys a bottle of champagne to toast their forty years. The waiter has balloons and a song. The husband is Italian, the waiter is Italian and suddenly it's the two tenors and a buoyant sense of bonhomie that could levitate us all. It has certainly elevated Emily who is on her feet and smiling and raising her glass to these people as if she has known them all her life. Oh and she means it, every word, right this minute and we are

all moved in a wonderfully irresponsible, no-strings-attached sort of way. And now the husband, the wonderful Italian halibut expert, is also on his feet and look he is going round to Emily's side of the table and there are violins, real violins playing. And here I know that if I were Emily I should have dropped the ball. I should have deferred graciously, insisted that the proper form be kept, that he dance first with his wife, and so would have spoiled everything and only drawn attention to a perceived gaffe where none occurred. I would have missed altogether the invitation to dance. But this is Emily, eighty-two and not about to miss a bonus turn, and she is taking his hand and he is sweeping her into a waltz while she says, Careful, careful, and his wife of forty years smiles and means it and applauds. I fumble with the camera. It isn't wound on and they are dancing round and round beside the table and she is looking up at him, his right hand expertly on the small of her back, his left enfolding hers. I take their picture as they turn and the camera whirs. It's the end of the roll.

Well. No one can top that. There is not much to say. I'm worrying about the dinner companion who purchased the champagne and the wife of course and was anyone buffeted by this extravagant display of gallantry? And the Suddenly-Subdued where have they gone? Oh let them be celebrating their own discoveries and please not angrily unscrewing the rye again.

Forster may have been right — *Only connect* — but he forgot to tell us how. There are the lucky few, the true fools, who need no teaching. They should be teaching us but would not dream of it. They are, they would say, just being themselves. They are worth watching.

When I get home I shall have the films developed. There will be rows and rows of misty mountains, steely water, rows and rows of pristine snow-capped peaks and bluer than blue bow-waves folding over on themselves, folding over. There will be only one that is dark and mistimed. I shall not be able to see the woman's face but I shall know that it is lit from within.

CATCH

*Outside the itself-constructed discourse on post-colonialism
and the deconstruction of hierarchies, on situatedness and
incommensurability, there is a whole fabric, a living network
just trying to make connections, just trying to get along. A
network — Jah rule — of i and i.*

IT'S DARK. Take your life in your hands to cross this narrow
ribbon of street where the traffic flies. Your children with
you, your life's blood, exulting in this frolic with death,
tickled to have burst the neat stitching of their Canadian
seams. Friday. Off to Oistins to the fish fry on this precipi-
tate Caribbean night that dropped like a fire-curtain over
the sunset while you were in the shower getting sand out
of your hair. Off to eat dinner under the stars with the
islanders. Who know how to live. But first to get there.
Narrow (no escape!), walled (monkeys behind that one)
road and a single-file-only sidewalk perilous with heaved
up slabs and broken curbs, rusty sign poles to ding you in
the head while you're watching your feet. Don't step off.
It's a game of hazard. Dicing with Mr. D . . . Jitneys passing
every few minutes, souped-up mini-vans swerving close to
scoop you if you want to be scooped. You do, you do. You
can't stand the tension. Wave one down. Better than being
hit by it. Number fourteen. Fourteen inside too — passengers — at least. No. Too many! Your voice competing with

40

the sound system while the conductor hauls your youngest in. "Too many?" He is incredulous. "How many you? Six? Yes, man. Is room. Get in. GET IN!" Oh you obedient white people clambering in over legs and thighs. Excuse me. Excuse me. Twenty of you now, not counting the crew of two, crammed in this steel capsule hell-bent on the fish market.

The onslaught of headlights in rapid succession flares in your consciousness. Eidetic: "applied to an image that revives an optical impression with hallucinatory clearness." This pot-holed street is two-way. The only way your driver can negotiate the blind corners and maximize on fares is with unyielding nerve. You have to laugh at the speed. Sometimes your mate and the other taller passengers hit their heads on the roof. Why it's padded with deep blue vinyl quilting. Painted with silver stars. You're not sure where the rest of your party are. Too tightly-packed to turn. Cramp already. The driver stops for two more fares, British tourists, then — time to give up all neuroses — another three. "I'm going to lose my kneecap on that door handle." Your voice addressed to no-one in particular has found a higher register. A voice as sweet and melting as rum-cake replies. "Don' worry, dahlin'. You got another one."

Flying the dark street, horn bellowing, West Indian beat blasting. Padded roof a plus if you roll over. Hot wind through the open window. Foreign smell of coconut oil, eucalyptus. Your daughter further back causing comment among the other passengers, muffled laughter but still super-polite. "You smell nice." She's asphyxiating everyone with her hair products, her own foreign smells. Then the road suddenly wider, lights appearing, a space station after an intrepid odyssey. A bright little mall on one side,

coconut palms and the dark sea on the other. Unfold your
limbs, unpack your wedged bodies and step out into the
velvety blacker-than-black. Soft boom of waves on the
beach. A Kentish accent from your childhood. "Ta-ta, then,
love. Look after them knees."

*Early next morning I take a walk along the newly washed sand
and think about that voice that summoned the accents of home,
my uncle's voice mixing with the traffic and the sea and the chorus
of peepers — the tiny tree frogs that thrive in the coleus.* My uncle
has lived all his life in the same gritty English town, taken his
holidays in the same quiet county. He left the country once, on
active service to France in 1940. It seemed to finish him for
"abroad", as shrapnel might, lodged in you like a stubborn memory.
What would he have made of the cheerful hodge-podge in the jitney?
He would have loved it. Marvellous, really, the way these
people get along. *Does it matter that he won't know their easy
hospitality, tropical night air, turquoise sea, the rattle of palm
fronds? I don't know. Is it range of experience, or depth, for which
we will give thanks at the end of our lives? Perhaps my uncle has
gained more from his Sikh neighbours than he ever could have from
a visit to the Punjab. I shan't have known many things: the sides
of Mount Kilimanjaro, the noise of Cairo, the land ocean of the
Gobi desert. For someone who believes the planet is hers to love,
honour and cherish for the duration of her life, I shall have seen
precious little of it when I die.*
    *And "seen" is the word. What I'm doing here in the West Indies,
on this Windward Isle, is mainly seeing, with once in a while a
little bit of knowing thrown in. I've stopped at the water's edge where
the fizzing surf performs a vanishing act. Through the soles of my
feet I can feel each faceted crystal of sand grinding against every
other under pressure of my weight. My heels can hear the minute*

squeaking and scratching. And I know this water, this sand, as I know my own skin. Time to dive in.

You've avoided ending as road-kill, you've survived the bus and reached the haven, both park and boat-yard, on the other side of the road. Catch your breath in the warm wind that blows straight from Africa, pouring across the dark sea (night-time all the way) to sweep up the beach and bend these skinny palms.

Tall fishing boats with flaking paint loom out of the darkness, tilt drunkenly on rusted oil drums. Faded blue, pale pink. Ghosts of themselves at sea. Underfoot, creeping grass with roots like flattened centipedes in the sand. Palm fronds rustling above. Air in motion riding the boats. The palm trunks bowed to match the stems of the fishing boats. Same graceful curve. Out to sea the darkness splits repeatedly here, there, to horizontal flashes of foam. It folds them into itself. In and under, swallowing moonlight. Your party navigates the boat-yard like its own regatta. Can't wait to get out of the picturesque peeling pathos. Give them a living crowd.

Through the covered fish market first at high speed, stepping over snaking red rubber hoses. You try to take in the stalls (seeing, seeing!). Red-tiled holding tanks filled with crushed ice for each vendor's fish. Buckets of fish heads. Stacks of newspapers. Reek of guts. Handsome slick-bodied fish: marlin, swordfish, dolphin-fish they assure you is not dolphin, tuna. Small flying fish interleaved in mounds. Ocean of plenty. To buy by the dozen. Nonchalant expertise and precision of the filleting. Tiny skeletal systems flicked out entire with the tip of a blade. The rest of your party has vanished now. Drawn like bees to the heaving hive of where it's at, the music, the bars and the barbecues in the open area where the lights are brighter. Oh, the exchange of money. It's what life's about: stuff to buy. Stalls there selling coconut bead chokers, shell necklaces, anklets, sarongs, wallets, T-shirts, beer, french fries. And fish, remember? We came here for dinner, remember?

Part rave, part fairground, the blacktop hosts a self-generating party. Kids dancing to a bone-blasting beat from two big speakers. A DJ mixing hip-hop, dub. Country music wailing from the bars. Stick a Banks beer in your hand and enter the enchanted circle of naked light bulbs strung on the wooden food stalls around the parking lot; Chez Daniel, Albert's Chicken Hut. Albert's whole family in there, two sons, wife, Grandma peeling onions at the back. The lit tableau repeated many times: Pattie's Pantry, The Fish Bucket, Sammy 'N' Tammy's. These are the side-shows to the main event, the great flaring barbecues of the fish fry itself. Drifts of light grey smoke, acrid and appetizing gust across from the open fires. Your eyes sting. You've gone deaf and it's OK. Elaborate cross-currents in the air, a mingling of sound and smell, onions, fish, tobacco, spatter, laughter, hiss, guitar chords, charcoal, sweat, after-shave, bass beat, beer. On the ground, the crowd's own pattern of swirls and eddies round the long line-ups inching toward the fires. Hook your family onto one like a segment of tape-worm. You can't see the beginning but since it's the longest it must — this surely a universal truth — lead to the hottest fire, the tastiest fish.

Aquamarine. Every morning the sea makes an offer I can't refuse. Only two other purposeful Northern types this morning. One walker, one swimmer. Out here in their own private oneness with the universe. The cool-warm water is scrupulously regulated by sun and wind to maintain the perfect swimming temperature. The steeply shelving beach creates a trough with a strong swell just behind the line of breakers. To swim its length it is to be cradled in a rhythm that lifts, that lets fall. The sea knows Zen!

Along the beach a power boat has washed ashore. I let a wave carry me in and walk over to take a closer look. The boat must have lain there all night, filling with sand and water, her bow driven into the sand bank left by the turning tide, canopy snapped off by the surf. "Hungover" painted on her hull. I go down the sea again. When I look back to check the location of the boat, two men have already arrived. They scratch their heads and kick at the gunwale as if it's a tire.

Swim back. In a little while the fruit seller will come by the beach-front apartments, balancing her impossible load of fresh produce on her head. How to rid the mind of stereotypes when they come walking up the beach? She carries a machete and will peel and slice a pineapple with it. She works there where she stands, holding and twirling the pineapple with one hand, taking off the bossed skin with deft strokes. She carves a triangular prism down round the flesh and the conical spines come out in one neat spiral. We'll eat the fruit later outside on the patio with a flurry of little birds hoping for a taste.

In Western consciousness, shaped by news broadcasts, the machete, the Collins it's called here, is always a weapon. I begin to wonder how the world might change if pineapple preparation were reported on the news instead of the hacking off of limbs. The fellow outside the supermarket uses a machete to thwack off the end of a coconut so that thirsty shoppers can purchase a drink for a few cents. He's there every day with his sack of coconuts, his bicycle and the growing pile of vegetative waste at the kerb. It can't provide much of a living but he doesn't seem unduly stressed by the fact.

The lad who works the beach makes more. He carries aloe leaves and empty mickies in a nylon British Airways flight bag circa 1960. He seeks out the new arrivals turning — though they don't know it yet — bright pink from over-zealous sun-bathing. A bottle of fresh aloe for fifteen dollars. It's a done deal as soon as his target discovers the flash of vermilion on the thigh, the hectic fuschia on the shoulder. He splits a leaf and scrapes the viscous jelly out. Aloe leaves were designed by God to funnel their juices neatly into the narrow necks of empty Mount Gay rum bottles. The plants grow freely, vigorously at the back of the beach and since the empty bottles are free the lad must be making one hundred percent on every sale. He'll stay to tell a few unlikely stories on the lines of being flown to London by the Body Shop; he'll offer to apply the product if you fall into the right demographic.

It's the women among the vendors who show more signs of stress. Everywhere there is beach life there are market stalls with racks of brightly coloured skirts and sarongs blowing out against the blue. The competition lends a coersive edge to the women's sales pitch. Perhaps it's the urgency of the mother who must go home after a day of these dallying, shilly-shallying tourists to find dinner for a houseful of children, to get their school shirts washed and dried, bleached shell-white and crisp for the next day. And we're dithering over the mauve or the red. If I was in their shoes, knowing the price of an air fare, I'd soon lose patience. Oh for the dear Lord's sake why you don't jus' give me a twenty an' stop maulin' me clothes?

You've inched nearer the barbecue and it looks like a good one. Three men wearing tank tops and bandannas work over fierce grills to sear the fish. Three women serve it on paper plates with rice and peas. The fires flare constantly and you can feel the heat from way back. This is no barbecue. It's a conflagration. Smoke rises from the spitting oils. A chalkboard: *Kingfish, Flying Fish, Tuna.* Every trestle table jammed shoulder to shoulder with tourists and locals. Foreign accents spiking the Bajun lilt. Birmingham, Cardiff, Glasgow. A few Aussies. A few Canadians. The odd German. The line stalls. You've finished your beer. Send your fifteen-year old off for more. You're bonding with your young over alcohol. No one here without a chilled beer in hand, except those with rum. This is a fairground, we the entertainment. Three middle-aged white women in front of you with a bottle of Malibu and three paper cups. Near the end of their stay, with limbs not white at all but medium brown. They make you want to stop going to the convent to write, start prowling. Muscular tanned arms and coarse bottle-bleached hair. One in a sarong, another in shorts and halter top with her hair in corn rows, thick veins purpling the backs of her knees. The third, the queen, in a short turquoise dress. Luvvly colour. Jus' like the sea. A tight sheath, horizontally creased, with spaghetti straps and a slit up the back. She's wearing it with stiletto sandals, a rhinestone strap across the toe. Yes, you'd like to be the queen. "Cougars," whispers your daughter in awe, and you achieve a rare communion.

The women place their order and you're next. A fluster of decisions, a crescendo of flame and hiss from the grill. From sea to grill to plate. You can't do this at home. Find a space at a table. Cram in. Your seared kingfish flakes and falls apart under your plastic fork. Just like an ad. Hot, hot, hot. Tender. You have become a family of wolves.

The women are at the next table. Finished already. The one in shorts splits away from the group. Starts to dance in front of the line-up, cradling her plastic cup. Dances herself further off, distancing herself in pretended self-absorption. To show how her hips move. Hoping to catch an admiring glance, or better, a lustful one. Spur some hapless male to groan under his breath, make a move. Her eyes flick up — just flick — scan the scene quickly to see who's looking. But it's only your scruffy family, mesmerized.

There's a moment after the swim. The sun is warm but not hot enough to burn. The beach is still empty. I belong to this air this sea this sky this sand. This day of my life belongs to me. Before the family's needs — and my own — kick in, there is a hiatus, the moment of lack. Monks submit themselves to long and arduous training for this.

"You like to swim." As if I've conjured him, a Rastafarian with dreads to the middle of his back is squatting on his heels beside me.

"Yes, I love to swim." It's a connection.

It's all the hint he needs. "You a vegetarian, right? Yoga? You know yoga." We have a fine conversation about body and soul and then he moves off a little way to do his sun salutations and stand on his head.

When I go inside for breakfast my husband laughs. Says I am merely the conduit to our eldest daughter. You think she's gone unnoticed out there? Well, of course he might be right. But I'd still like to think we made a connection and it wasn't about sex, or ganja. And perhaps I should allow the dancing woman last night a little latitude. Perhaps she was just at home in the music. Just being. Like the middle-aged man with a portable CD player. He set it up near the bars, put on "Stand By Your Man" and began to dance. He was in his fifties and wore brown slacks, mustard shirt with a long collar, and a grey tweed cap. He danced by himself soliciting partners from the small crowd that quickly gathered. A woman in a yellow dress joined him, beaming. They danced hip to hip in a tight ballroom embrace. They might have known each other forever. The spectators made a close circle, barely gave them room to move.

Time to leave the table to the next in line. Cruise the scene. The bars filling up for the night. Mad Michaelz Watering Hole. Flimsy wooden clapboard. Would fly to Kansas in a hurricane, no problem. The Glass Bottom. This one is larger, a dance hall. Stools at narrow counters round the open sides. Patrons settling in for the evening, getting primed. Some of them there already. Johnny Cash has commandeered the night. The floor in the centre crowded with swaying bodies. Outside, on the side facing the ocean, older men at card tables, deaf to the whumping and the pumping and the twang from inside, smack dominoes down with conviction. They have their own crowd around them, intent on the game. Oblivious to noise and jostle. Oblivious to appetite. Could be on an empty beach under the palm trees, or under the bread-fruit tree on the corner of the village cross road. Oblivious to you, too. Live advertisement for over-consumption that you are, you don't exist.

You could stay a little longer, go into the bar, have (yet) another beer. But it's their home turf, their territory. You'd be a blot, a blight with your greedy eyes touring the room. You head back through the boat-yard, under the flaking hulls. The wind picks up the music and sweeps it inland. It's already distant. You flag down a jitney. Room to breathe in this one. Sit up front. Check the speed. Needle at zero, flips to sixty and back again over bumps. You'll be home too soon. You want the salt wind again and the black sea. Stop the driver ahead of time. Get out to walk the rest of the way on the beach. Ignore the protests of dissenters. Soft crash of waves on your left. Bright foam flowering and melting away. And something moving. Everything moving. The sand everywhere alive with a phantom scuttling. Your daughters indulge in girly shrieking as long-legged crabs appear and vanish back down their tunnels. You see more and more as your eyes adjust to the dark. They are every-where, these ghost crabs. You are a walking incursion, giants in Lilliput wreaking havoc and doom. Self-induced hysteria — on both sides. The crabs vanish noiselessly into their tunnels while you pass in a raucous din.

I swim on and off throughout the day, Afternoons are busiest. More people on the beach, more activity in the water, though not much of it involves swimming. It's prime time. I like the crowds further along where the surf is strong enough to take you up the beach on a boogie board, not quite high enough for surfers to take your head off. In the big hotel at the back they're setting up a bandstand and firework display for Saint Patrick's day. I'm doing nothing much at all. Just floating in a little piece of reclaimed day. Just being. I've been thinking about all this booze. We're awash in it here. Can polish off a bottle of rum in no time. When we go back we'll try to replicate the sundown drink with our cherished duty-free. It won't work. Rum and coke here on the beach while the sand turns to pink and the palms darken is pure nectar. But it's baguette and cheese in France, sardines and tomatoes in Spain. It doesn't travel. Just as well. We would all be in rehab in no time.

In this land of sugar cane, alcohol is promoted tirelessly and shamelessly. Peddled to visitors and residents alike: in elegant displays of Malibu and Mount Gay in Cave Shepherd's shiny downtown store and without ceremony in all the little bars, the sugar shacks that operate on so many street corners out of town.

*White clapboard shops with a front that lifts up to form an awning,
these bars don't have a sign outside. They are the sign, appropri-
ated lock, stock and barrel by Banks beer whose logo — the black
silhouette of a dancing rastaman — gesticulates exuberantly across
their entire exteriors, sometimes extending over the roof. (My mother
used to keep a beaming black mammy on the kitchen wall — a
plaster Aunt Jemima figure with a notepad for an apron. She was
a far cry from the fruit vendor who, for whatever reason, has not
cracked a smile yet. The dancing rasta is just as far removed from
the old fellows who sit inside these bars watching cricket on TV or
filling the air with the companionable click of dominoes while they
drink.) Alcohol is conspicuous at every major event from the Test
Match to the harvest festival of Cropover. It's touted by all the hotels
and clubs who try to ensure by their promotions — all drinks a
dollar on Tuesdays; twenty dollars 'membership' on Wednesday
and drink all night for free — that you'll get yourself hammered
on every night of the week.*

*A couple wade into the sea close by and stand waist deep
talking. A young Brit and a Barbadian girl. She's wearing a brand
new bikini in a shiny metallic fabric, pale blue. Perhaps she brought
it expressly for this. He's talking to her in a way that's both eager
and tentative at the same time. Courting! That was a mating
dance last night. This is courting. Polite, attentive. He hasn't
entered her world yet. He talks to her from a vast distance. Choosing
his words with deliberate care as if she speaks another language,
he is explaining carefully, about St. Patrick's Day. "Do you know
what that is? In our country, well, not in my country but in
Ireland, over there, the people celebrate St. Patrick's Day because
St. Patrick is their patron saint. Over there." She smiles. "Oh, I
see." Not far from the beach, McBride's pub has been advertising
St. Patrick's Night for the last ten days. He nods towards the
breakers. "Swim, then?'" — and ploughs in. She hangs back,*

flinching at the splashes, meticulously timid. He calls to her. "Come on out here. Do as you're told." He makes a point of laughing straight away, a little too soon, just to be sure she'll know it's a joke. And she laughs back, a little too loud, so he'll know she has a sense of humour.

MINE! MINE! MINE!

THE TROUBLE WITH NOVELS is not only that they take so long to read, while the time available to read them diminishes correspondingly, but that they take so excruciatingly long to write. All sorts of changes occur in the four of five years it takes to write one. You change, your ideas evolve. Your plot falls apart, then your family, then you, your computer. You go off (big time) your main character, then your in-laws. A hole appears in the ozone. Most of this you can accommodate. Change is natural. Change is good. It's only when your book is unwittingly usurped — or anyway a scene from it, or anyway an idea, or anyway your protagonist's middle name, or the colour of his underwear — that you really go into a tail spin.

My husband said, after he showed me the ad in *Saturday Magazine*, that he had not heard me bellow quite like that since the birth of our first child. He said he had thought twice about showing me: a half page colour shot of a diver leaving the top board and poised in mid-air over a perfect reflection of limitless sky. The rest of the page was taken up with the image of a fat Swiss watch and, blazoned above it, the very words I had chosen as the title for my next book. He also said I shouldn't bang my head down on the desk like that. He said he didn't think it was *that* important. Well, no. And arsenic isn't *that* poisonous and World War II wasn't *that* big and spontaneous combustion wouldn't be fatal. To have your own title slapped on the cover of another writer's book is (believe me) bad enough but to have its appearance on a billboard beside the highway or see it flashed across the screen in the middle of the Showcase Revue . . .

To appreciate the depth of feeling involved here you have to understand that such incidents have the potential to cast doubt on the very foundations of what writers do. Creativity R us. Don't ever suggest we do anything other than spontaneously ignite with our magnificent, unique flame of inspiration. We delude ourselves that we take the long view from our observation towers but that only makes the slap of reality harder when we belly flop in the common stream. This strange blindness — not seeing ourselves as part of the experiment that is humanity — only makes the shock of recognition more jarring when it does arrive.

There is a strange confluence of ideas constantly at work in a culture and I've been caught in the eddies often. It works like letters to MPs. If an idea or an image catches in your imagination then you can guarantee it will have kindled the minds of at least a hundred other creators.

My book *The Turning* was particularly plagued. It came out in 1996. It opens with a shipwreck (Jane Urquhart) that dumps an Englishman (Michael Ondaatje, Guy Vanderhague) on the coast of France (Sebastian Faulks) where he falls in love with a photographer (Kathleen Govier) who witnesses a nasty nautical misadventure (Jane Campion) and finishes by losing an extremity (Stephen King). Its title by the way was *The Crossing* until a month before publication when . . . (Cormack McCarthy). Enough said. You would think I had my ear to the ground or at least my nose in the Saturday supplements for the duration of the novel, when in fact I live in a kind of hermetically sealed bubble when I'm writing, the outside world only occasionally leaking in.

What is a writer to do? To take evasive action and alter anything along the way would be to give the process a different spin altogether, something in the nature of a parlour game: an Englishman/Irishman/Canadian is shipwrecked/falls from a plane/is fishing for cod off the coast of France/New South Wales . . . The only sensible course is to keep your head down and carry on scribbling, like a war correspondent in the trenches.

Occasionally the whole process works in reverse. Two years after *The Turning* with its photographer and its background of the Franco-Prussian war, Beryl Bainbridge in England came out with a tale featuring a photographer in the Crimean war. I was so delighted by many of the similarities, thrilled to think that a writer I admire had seen the same possibilities in this material, that I naively wrote to her. Not surprisingly, she never replied but then she's had her own problems, having her tour de force novel of the Titanic, *Every Man For Himself* swamped by the James Cameron movie.

Every writer likes to think she is working in her own territory, beyond the borders of the over-tilled fields that make up our shared contemporary consciousness — some thorny scrubby area that will eventually yield not the boring old peas and carrots but some extraordinarily rare and monstrously beautiful fruit, kumquats and pomegranates at the least. But here is the strange thing: you bend your back and hoe and till and sow and water and hoe again and when you look up there are all around you a dozen more, hoeing and tilling and working the same patch, your patch.

For many years I had a pathological fear of reading the writers I most admired lest I should find my hard-won ideas already brilliantly treated, nothing left to be said. I deprived myself of a wealth of fine writing. And then I read P.K. Page's collection *Hologram*. In her introduction, P.K. refers to the work of an ornithologist who discovered that song birds reared in isolation were able to sing, albeit imperfectly; but when exposed to the songs of other birds, of other species, they were able to take the notes they needed to complete their own song.

The currency of ideas is not of course confined to writing. There's a mechanism at work in any culture that operates, as Kalle Lasn has patiently explained, something like a virus or a gene. Richard Dawkins, Lasn tells us, first coined the term 'meme', referring to any idea or fad or piece of information that latches on to a host to be conducted at high speed throughout an entire social consciousness. I call it Plague syndrome. It's teen fashion for the mind. Think of those apocryphal divorce revenge tales, feng shui, the word "Not!", Monica Lewinski jokes, acts of random kindness, cherubs, St. John's Wort, "Hel*lo-oo*!" Make your own list. What's more, as far as I can see (from my place in the stream) there are also mega memes at work, the most recent of which is metaphysical. First there were angels, which were in the ascendant for quite a while before they began to plummet and finally met their nadir in Hallmark. Then it was the soul. There was a time when the soul was the particular province of Catholics. Every good, and bad, Catholic had one of her own to lug around, spotted or not. Now that everyone has one, some people are acquiring a spirit as well and buying hand made soaps and bath oils to care for it. It may not be long before we see furry Soulbies and gossamer sprites marketed along with scented candles. (Just remember that that intellectual (*sic*) property is mine . . .)

And on the subject of intellectual property, the luxury to whine about perceived appropriation of one's own may soon come to an ugly end. A writer friend had the reckless notion, one week before publication, to look up her new title on the internet, "just to see". Well she saw it — already in use by a writer in the states. There is no copyright at present on titles (for who would want a used one?) and she resolved the problem readily with a new title. Still, it's only a matter of time before titles, like aphorisms or proverbs or biblical phrases will begin to slide out of the public domain and into the realms of private, for-profit, holdings. E-speculators have already begun mining the riches of our language, squatting fatly with their "rights" on the beautiful pasture of words that you and I hold in common for us and for our heirs.

I suppose I can think myself lucky that there was no ominous "TM" after the phrase that will be my title. Then it *would* have been "*that* important" and touched more than a bruised ego. As it is, I'll put my head down again and get back to scribbling.

Titles and ad copy aside, I know I may still bump up against other writers exploring the same territory I'm working. But now I hope I'll be able to work happily beside them, knowing that for an artist in for the long haul none of it matters; each work stands — and lives or dies — on its own merits; each work has its own internal logic and cohesion, its own integrity.

Any editor who has ever put out a call for anthology submissions on a single theme understands this process.

What she gets in the mail are not five hundred versions of the same theme but five hundred wildly diverse, mystifyingly various and variegated surprises. Of course more than one artist can work the same ground. Of course. The seeds of the imagination, at least for as long as we resist cloning ourselves, are organic, our production is not genetically uniform, and every writer reaps her own strange harvest.

And mine? The harvest of my title? Oh, right, I'll tell you. As if.

GETTING THE HORSE IN THE BARN

ON FINISHING HER THIRD NOVEL, Daphne Du Maurier wrote that it had taken her nine months: "all the labour of having a child. I drank its health in sloe gin!" No question that she plucked the right metaphor there, but where did that blithe breeziness come from? What happened to the pain and the tears?

I know how it's done by the rest of us. Watch mothers leaving their young on the first day of Kindergarten — clasping, squeezing, lingering, turning back. One more word, one more look. That's how the novelist parts with the manuscript.

I find it so hard to do, I delivered my last novel in person to my agent. Even then I couldn't hand it over but sat with it, the infant on my lap, through lunch. It was only wrested from my grasp when, lunch over, I was heading for the door, the manuscript still, to our mutual embarrassment, under my arm.

It's difficult to let go of a book after living with it for . . . how long? Certainly longer than nine months. John Fowles wrote that he loathed the day he had to send a manuscript to the publisher "because on that day the people one has loved die". Difficult to let go but, oh, so easy to forget how ghastly the confinement. For your creation is a pregnancy. A long one, endured in a prison of your own making. You forget how terrible. The infant, your cell mate, appears about halfway through term — your "time". It grows bigger, uglier and more demanding every day until it has finally taken up all the space in your head, your heart, your life — what you had left of it. You dream of freedom.

Five years! Six! Cooped up with the obnoxious monster-child. Sometimes you wake in the small hours, listen to its breathing, assure yourself that it still lives. But on the bad nights you lie sleepless in a torment of doubt and mistrust. This Thing will be the death of you.

So it's a thrilling prospect, nearing the end of your sentence. The book is written and all that's left is to tidy the final draft. Even then you find yourself adding another twenty pages, another ten. Another sentence. You lunge for the door crying "Air!" when it's over.

The love-hate paradox is the predicament of every mother. And every writer. The desire to bear children arrives with the force of an earth-mover. It will not be deflected. And then you have them. They grow, elbowing you and your puny life into the corner beside the fridge, treading you thin as a door mat (but still you would die for them). You teach them, you think, to take wing, show them how, you think. But look! There they are, their size ten-and-a-halfs still planted firmly, and you still feeding them just one last bowl of nutritious (alphabet!) soup.

I've heard the process of raising teenagers likened to the birth process. "You push and you push and finally they're out the door." It holds for novels too. No wonder we can't resist hitting the caps key and typing E N D when the final word is entered — though we'll still clutch them at the open door.

Is every art form as enervating? I doubt it — which is not to imply any correlation between pain and merit. The particular difficulties of finishing a novel are inherent in the form itself and exacerbated by the very technology that has, in other ways, made it so much easier to write. To begin with, the form is open ended. This is not true of the short story, nor of the essay, both closed forms. You know the instant these are complete in themselves and you certainly know when they are not. Your way forward is always relatively clear. Other forms, the poem in almost all its varieties, most strikingly haiku, are roundly, soundly closed — for the writer. A successful poem may be open to interpretation from the reader. It may, probably should, overflow with potentiality. But for the poet the affair is over. There was only one poem to write, only one way to write it.

With a novel, choices are more or less infinite. Mostly more. You may begin with the birth of your character, end with his death. Or the other way round. Or you can begin with his Mum and end with her death. Or begin with his Mum's death. You can start if you like with the birth of Christ. Or Buddha. You can travel six, seven generations from the now of the novel and end in another century — which is what it feels like by the time you get there.

Because it's multi-dimensional, the novel behaves like crazy expanding foam. It's the mousse that swells from the aerosol, the fairy-tale porridge that boils through the town. Not only *can* it extend its reach forward and back in time, it can expand widthways and amplify the now. You can add as many details of time and place as you wish (and some writers do). Think about it: as many. Or take the vertical view. Everything you touch on in every other direction can be stretched vertically. Not only can be stretched but demands to be. Characters clamour for moral attributes, psychological, emotional; landscape wants a piece of the drama; even your inanimate players are hankering after their proper cultural, social and political significance.

The question of point of view opens a whole new set of options. It's not enough to have a room of your own. Insist on a chaise longue too. You will need to lie down. Often.

A room of your own, a chaise longue and preferably a half dozen legal pads, a packet of pencils, and a sharpener. Computers make certain tasks (most of them to do with entering words, almost none of them to do with thinking) immeasurably easier — others almost insurmountably harder. Chunks of text become floating building blocks. You can move them around as necessary — but you can also move them just for the hell of it. Switch enough of them often enough and the hacienda you thought you were building starts to look like a high-rise, or your corporate head-quarters a cluster of cabanas.

Moving text with ease starts out as an advantage but tack this capability onto the novel's multi-dimensionality and you've multiplied your problems exponentially. The writer who actually sits at the keyboard to create a first draft had better know exactly where her novel is going and have a firm grip on the technology that is taking it there. If not, the desktop folder that contains (ha!) the novel will soon be filled with a jumble of drafts, many of which will look identical on opening, their baffling labels no help at all. You can see how technology might actually add to the discomfort of your long confinement. It's serious work, and a drain on creative energy, too, tracking this volume of material. The worst of it is that after three hundred pages' of composition you will not necessarily be three hundred pages nearer the end. The novelist learns the hard way to use the computer's power sparingly.

Annie Dillard, discussing the writing process, has pointed out a fact so obvious it usually draws no remark: that writing proceeds across the page, word after word, leaving a visible trail. The painter, she says, on the other hand, covers over her first strokes, so that the finished painting overlays the earlier attempts. Now with this in mind it seems to me that the computer might be a handy tool for painting — one screen overlaying another — but that it's utterly at odds with the process of writing. The last thing you want as a writer is to have your first pages obscured in this way. No use scrolling back to look — you won't be able to see what you wrote a moment ago. Use a split screen? You'll still need to hold the intervening text in your head. No, you'll have the pages fanned out in an extravagant semi-circle, or perhaps a large sensuous 'S' over the bedroom floor — the bedroom being, by this stage of the novel, with the writer's partner thoroughly alienated, the room least likely to invite disturbance.

Only the physical pages can show a writer the true shape of her book — and how close she is to that elusive end. They can reveal other essential intelligence, as well, information to do with the proportion and the rhythm and drive: how one section is carrying too much weight in relation to its role in the narrative, how another needs a stronger link, another more force.

The physical pages are your first defence against that inherent problem of choice. The special properties of longhand composition can perform little miracles no computer programme has yet mastered. Text hand-written and double spaced on legal bond with amendments between the lines, in the margins, over the top and in red, in green, in that inviting space at the bottom, can show you all the possibilities at once. You can even write diagonally across the text and still read both versions. It might be messy but when you look back you see at a glance the choice you have to make. Often you'll scratch the losers through (though you will not of course have "lost" them — an additional benefit) before you've even turned the page. Given that this novel/monster-baby/cellmate is as intractable and demanding as it is, you need a few miracles.

The day comes of course, though you thought it never would, when the cell door flies open and . . . and that wrenching sound is coming from your heart. It's done, finished, over. Everywhere else there is a terrible silence. You can barely remember the labour pains. But here is the strangest part — you discover that "out there" is a whole lot smaller than you remember it. Your tiny, dark, cramped cell was nothing less than a world containing all space, all time. And you really did "do" time in your cell. You morphed it and warped it and tied it in knots. On a good day you made it stand still. And it felt wonderful. No choice but to take up the pen again.

❖

None of these observations on the labour of creation fully explains why — apart from the form's constraints, or more accurately their lack — the novel is such a reluctant and laggardly finisher. Why, when you've written the tale, tied up the plot and killed off half your characters, doesn't the creature prick up its ears, whinny, and head, as a writer friend puts it, for the barn?

One of the things that happens to a novel under construction (to keep these metaphors moving) is that the builders keep walking off the job and a fresh crew takes over. The novel you finish is not in the same hands as the one you started. It has in effect a new author. Two things have changed you. The first is the simple act of writing it. You know more about whatever it was that first impelled you to build a novel: beauty, carnage, your Aunt Ada, shipwrecks, guppies; you know less — that is, you have more questions — about other things: love, death. Nearly always those. You entered at chapter one, and five, six years later you graduated.

The second change is due directly to the passage of time. In six years, trends have come and gone, as have threats to world peace, offers of advancement, new books, the Olympics, world so-called leaders. Your family may have come — or gone — in six years. No one remains untouched by the world. Even in your cell you had a radio, you had visitors.

But while these changes may account for the compulsion to keep adding material, they still don't get to the heart of the matter and tell us what this reluctance to let go is all about. It may well be the same as the impulse to begin. There's something deeply hidden in both.

We write because we have questions, not answers. If I turn back to the notes I made at the start of that stubborn novel six years ago, I see only reachings, falterings. They begin literally, with a question. Here's the very first entry, verbatim:

> The bliss of the cloud scene comes near the
> end, last quarter. It works towards peace. It
> *leads* somewhere. It represents continuity,
> eternity, transcendence?? It casts back to
> *dis*harmony of earlier procession/cloud
> scene.

This is not planning or plotting. This is groping forward with the lights off. But although the remarks seem to be technical jottings on the process of building, they're really echoing the larger questions that drive the entire process. That third sentence, "It *leads* somewhere", with its pathetic, blind yearning might express the motivation for all writing.

Rilke, who used the birth analogy freely for the creative process, saw the creative experience and the sexual as "unbelievably close . . . different forms of the same longing and bliss."

And here's Northrop Frye, with tighter focus: "the story of the loss and regaining of identity is the framework of all literature."

And, with brilliance, Gertrude Stein, "Time and identity are what you create only when you create they do not exist."

The lost state is really an alternative state, accessible to all of us the moment we allow the created world in. It's the living we do when we're stopped in our tracks by a sky on fire, or when, walking or swimming, our cells flood with remembrance. We get it, that union — that communion, sometimes — from the eyes of our lovers, our children. We don't get it enough.

The grittiness of the world rubs and scrubs away at the sublime in us, thins it out until we begin to doubt its existence. It's the search for proof of it, this elusive condition, that is the impulse for much of our art and the depiction of the struggle for it that is the business of so many novels. The disaffected protagonist contends with the forces of society — Communism, an ex-girlfriend, globalization, the National Rifle Association — that keep him or keep her from the place of oneness. It can be oneness with a Supreme Being, a lover, Nature, himself, herself, a Canada Goose. It doesn't matter. What matters is the experience of it, which the novelist through the protagonist tries constantly to reaffirm. We're destined to return again and again to the well. It's the sense that there is *some*thing, that sweetest sip, that deepest kiss, just out of reach that keeps us coming back, or never wanting to leave.

And of course it's unattainable. Like a poem, this experience will not be called down. It will only descend. But that never stopped any of us from trying.

In desperation, when I was nearing the end of my book and could, as my friend said, smell the barn, I took my lead from the painter Géricault. The book tarried, and so close to home. I realised I was not wanting to let it go, hoping perhaps that if I held on to it I might catch just one more glimpse of the sky on fire. When Géricault was having trouble with *The Raft of the Medusa* he is said to have shaved his head so that he would be forced to stay in his studio and finish. I didn't shave my head but it helped to stay in my pyjamas for a week and only go out for the mail. It helped, too, to know that there *is* no end to the search. That the journey will begin again.

ANNE HÉBERT

*"On the river, in the fields and the woods, birth and death
reign in equal measure"*

NOT LONG OFF THE BOAT FROM TILBURY TO MONTRÉAL (a Russian
boat, it occurs to me now, the *Alexander Pushkin,* whose
identity fits nicely if meaninglessly with what is to follow)
and appointed to a teaching position on the other side of
the country, I asked the school secretary — possessed of
by far the brightest mind in the school — which authors I
should read if I wanted to get in touch with Canadian
Literature. She answered at once with what I still regard as
impeccable judgement that the writer I needed to read if
I was looking for a great Canadian mind was Northrop
Frye. She said that as for novelists, Mordecai Richler was a
must and there were two Margarets. One was very good and
the other was a drag. She said if I was looking for a really
good story I should try the book she'd just finished by a
French-Canadian, Anne Hébert.

The cover of my 1974 PaperJacks edition of *Kamouraska*
presents a still from Claude Jutra's film adaptation of the
novel: a snowy landscape, black pines, a solitary house on
the horizon; in the foreground a woman, Geneviève
Bujold, wrapped in red wool against the cold, a man beside
her in the sleigh, a black bearskin on the seat behind:
white, red, black, the colour of fairy tale. The man and the

woman in deep delight with each other, with life. Unmistakably in love. I'd likely have pulled the book from the shelf at Duthie's without the recommendation. How could I resist? I had scarcely returned from several years of mind travel across the blood-spattered steppes of Russian literature. Another *troika*, another *dacha*? Refuse another sojourn in that landscape where humans are larger than life and passion is both sovereign and saviour, where volition is still a possibility? I bought the book.

I spent the first few pages trying to untangle the threads this French narrator was knitting between Quebec city, Montréal, Burlington and Kamouraska — a place that seemed strangely accessible for somewhere in Russia. Things became much clearer as soon as I had abandoned all thoughts of snowy steppes and Muscovites, clearer still once I had relinquished the Romantic lens.

In my defence I should say that I came across *Wuthering Heights* at a tender age; it's notoriously difficult to shake off early influences. Recovery from the Romantics is particularly painful. If you meet them at nineteen or twenty, you will come away relatively unscathed, at seventeen you will be severely wounded but recover. At fourteen or fifteen the blow is fatal.

Kamouraska may have all the ingredients of the Romantic novel — illicit love, a flirtation with folklore and the supernatural, a landscape imbued with crushing power, a crime of passion — but they are shaken and stirred in the flask of Hébert's twentieth century sensibility. "Let ourselves both be damned forever" may sound at first like a typical nineteenth century heroine with a death wish but in fact Elizabeth, plotting with her lover to kill her husband has a ruthlessness more in common with Lady Macbeth, who as we know was a thoroughly modern woman. "The time has come to split in two. Accept this total, sharp division of my being . . . Learning to leave my words and gestures far behind me. With no one any the wiser, no one to know how utterly empty they are." This is the heroine, coldly. No victim but a calculating woman with a manipulative will, capable of sacrificing all for what she most desires, yet choosing to instead to weigh the risks against her own survival. You would not want to be her wife; even her lover would do well to watch out. "I don't mind waiting here by the side of the road. (Like a sweet little child, lost in the snow.) Waiting for Antoine to be put to death. But don't think you'll make me follow you all the way . . . " We're far from *La Dame aux Camèlias*.

Nor will you find an omniscient narrator to settle you down by the fire for this tale. The narrator, her hair all awry, is busy tumbling down a snow bank with her lover, even while her corporeal self is lying semi-delirious in a darkened room. Step in here and you must make your own way among the slippery tenses, the whispering voices; pay attention or you'll find yourself face to face with the murdered husband. Anne Hébert makes no concessions to readers who want a bed-time story. Entering her books, you sign away your rights to a comfortable existence. The great Romantic writers had mapped their terrain and conducted a guided tour from their mahogany desks. We knew we were in good hands: they knew the way back. Even Emily Brontë — as C.P. Sanger first observed — was writing to a strictly schematized plan of her own making, constructing an elaborate, symmetrical set within which she moved her carefully balanced cast. We were never in danger from Heathcliffe; he was always Cathy's. But

Hébert's deft manipulation of voice and her use of direct address pulls us into her landscape where we bump up against her characters; we infiltrate their dreams, we experience their passions. In *Kamouraska* there's no fireside for us, no mahogany desk for the narrator. We go in company. Our guide claims no superior knowledge or moral ground. Elizabeth is created by a sensibility as modern as her reader's: "The way you tell a story. Not taking it too seriously, with an amused little smile. Even if happiness turns to vinegar, to bitter gall."

This is the only novel I can think of that comes close to achieving the protracted emotional drive that gave *Wuthering Heights* his power. It's a sustained act of the imagination realized through hard craft. Turn it which way you will, its integrity remains intact. It won the Paris Book prize and marked Hébert as a major writer of the twentieth century. That it was awarded no honours in Canada remains an unsolved crime of Canadian Literature.

❖

The House of Anansi website presents Anne Hébert as "one of Canada's most highly acclaimed and successful literary stars." True on both counts, though in English-speaking Canada, despite Anansi's stalwart championship, you would hardly know it. Drop her name without introduction into a literary discussion and your listener will turn her head slightly, narrow her eyes as if she can't quite put a face to the name. "Québec", you say, "*Kamouraska*" and a pale light of recognition will dawn, tentatively. The names of Edna O'Brien, Doris Lessing, Carson McCullers, none of them Canadian, might evoke a sharper image; certainly the names of Anne-Marie MacDonald or Anne Michaels will resonate, both of whom have been published as the next Best Thing but have yet to produce a body of work equivalent to Hébert's. Does the book industry (an ominous term if there ever was, suggestive of churning and clunking) have to sweep the shelves quite so assiduously every year?

Within Québec itself the work of Anne Hébert enjoys a prominent position in the literary landscape. The website *www.mlink.net* lists almost two hundred works devoted to her writing. The University of Sherbrooke houses the Centre Anne Hébert. In her lifetime she was received into both the Order of Canada and the Ordre National du Québec. Her work in French received three Governor General's Awards from Canada, and the Prix Femina (among others) from France. In English-speaking Canada her death occasioned a full page tribute on the front page of the *Globe and Mail Review*. Yet she remains inexplicably obscure, less recognizable than, say, Michel Tremblay, or Roche Carrier in our consciousness as readers. Why is this? It's easy to refute the language argument: we've never had any trouble with Flaubert after all (the reference is not flippant — more of him later); not only that, Hébert's work has in its favour the fine translations of Sheila Fischman, one could almost call them distillations since they are in their power one hundred percent proof, and in their clarity pure as ice water.

Perhaps our neglect of this writer is more complex. Thinking about the anomaly has drawn my attention to the very real nature of our two solitudes, and more. Since the 1970s our literature has been swept by successive waves of fashion tied either to identity — of place, of origin, of social grouping etc. — or to region. The two major waves in fiction, the high rollers (if we can sweep on a pun into the casino where analogies with publishing and marketing are particularly apt) have been prairie literature and more recently east coast writing, with continuing runs from Asian and immigrant communities accompanying them. So far, there has been no wave of First Nations fiction to win a popular readership or to dominate the literary pages for any length of time. The energies of First Nations writing, with the exception perhaps of Thomas King, have been concentrated in other areas, notably drama — Tomson Highway and Daniel David Moses — and poetry — Lee Maracle, Greg Schofield, among many others. The shortage of fiction should take no one by surprise. Drama and poetry have always been the strongest voices among people who have been marginalized or oppressed — and in cultures with a strong oral tradition. It might even be argued that a particular brand of racism, operating like an insidious computer bug or a kind of low-grade fever, has been responsible for corralling First Nations' creative talent in the acceptable (to whites) confines of traditional — outmoded and therefore irrelevant, therefore non-threat-ening — forms of expression. The lack of a distinct wave of First Nations fiction — that might help Canadians identify with both commonality and difference — is like a missing piece of the national puzzle, but you can see how it got lost.

More perplexing to me, especially given the prolific output from Canadian writers in French (there are nine hundred writers listed on *l'Île*, the website for Québec writers) is that French-Canadian literature, unless I've missed something, has not enjoyed its own run of popular favour. There's a discrepancy between its place in our consciousness and its output and quality. Is it a matter of simple economics, the increased cost to a publisher of a translation? Or is it that French-Canadian literature is both accepted and dismissed as foreign — a literature that has little to do with us. Its absence is our loss. Distinct it may be but Québec is a constituent of our cultural mosaic. Québec is part of my country (I'm speaking now of course as an arrogant Brit — fast becoming the only type of Brit that is allowed possible in twenty-first century Canada. But that's another essay). The people of Québec are my brothers and sisters and I want to know them better. I don't sense a groundswell of interest. I can't be the only one.

To put my intuition to the test, I began asking friends (with one exception, since she knew what I was working on) if they knew any novels by Anne Hébert. None did. Only my partner, who suffers the rampant profligacy of my books about the house, scored an 'A'. I decided to check with a few bookstores. I included Victoria's most venerable as well as its most maligned in my list. The phone response was the same in every case. Just as there is no disguising the fact that you're still in bed when someone calls at 7 AM, there was no disguising the blank space behind the polite reply: "Um — could you spell that, please?" I should have to ask not booksellers but actual readers. I devised a one-answer survey: How many novels of Anne Hébert can you name? I left it on a clipboard in the local library. It required nothing more than a check in the appropriate column. After three weeks or so there were two checks in the zero column — both of them entered by my children. In a last — and I am nothing if not persistent — effort to find a cognizant public for this writer, I decided to turned to a distinctly literate group and sent my survey by e-mail to members of the Federation of BC Writers. Its two hundred-odd membership yielded a dozen replies, of those only two or three broke the uniform response of "nil".

Anne Hébert's case is, to be sure, exceptional. Super-imposed on her professional persona is another layer of "foreign-ness"acquired through her decision to live most of her writing life in Paris, a decision that may have served to distance her work further. But what about Mavis Gallant? Gallant, her contemporary and friend, made the same decision, matched her book for book and prize for prize — and enjoys a considerably higher profile. Brian Moore, another expatriate, achieved a similar notoriety and was energetically celebrated as a Canadian writer on the strength of a short stay and a couple of books. But Gallant writes and Moore wrote in English. Which brings us back to the language question.

Despite the fact that we maintain two official languages; that French, where it is considered the official second language is a core subject in the schools; that French Immersion schooling is available in many regions, and that we maintain a national French televison channel and produce Francophone films, French is rarely, barely and poorly spoken by any except those who have reason to speak it in the home. Listen to any conversation between a Francophone and an Anglophone. It will be conducted in English. The fear of French that English Canadians exhibit is as common and as psychologically laden with dubious baggage as fear of flying.

Still, with access to excellent translations, it should not pose a problem. Most educated Canadians would be able to place Gustave Flaubert. What a pity then that his direct literary descendent is so little known. And how we deprive ourselves, for Anne Hébert is Flaubert's match in psychological insights, his equal in swift delivery of the dagger to the heart. Her fictions are as complete, as pared and as perfect as his *Trois Contes* — and in narrative technique she outstrips him, able to draw on all the literary developments of the twentieth century.

There's one more aspect to this case of literary neglect worth consideration. Mention it, the neglect, to other readers and they don't think it's surprising. Anne Hébert is French after all. Why would, should we be aware of her? It's the way we are. There's a lot of stuff going on in Québec. We can't know it all. It's life. What everyone means but what no one quite manages to say is that Québec is a foreign country. Such a closed attitude should, in the lurid glow of rising nationalisms across the world, sound an alarm. I'm not suggesting by any means that if we don't read Anne Hébert we'll come to blows. What I am suggesting is the continued existence of an overall mentality that erects barriers and that these barriers, once in place, are of the kind that few have the energy or the will to cross. Quarrels grow into blood feuds on just such calcified grounds of dismissal, isolation and exclusion. Are these thoughts outlandish? We've seen Europe reverting to the bloody squabbles of former centuries. And didn't we once see terrorism in Canada, or is that particular memory in exile under the far corner of the rug?

But the thought "foreign" is supposed to have been tossed in the pc laundry to be tumbled clean with the strong new detergents of difference and diversity and distinctness. Besides, one cannot be "foreign" in one's homeland. So now it is OK to think of Quebec as distinct — and then dismiss it?

Several factors conspire in Anglo-Canadian consciousness to keep the work of Anne Hébert (like that of Marie-Claire Blais, or Gaëtan Soucy and others) in the wings. I've already noted the most significant, her "Frenchness" and her decision to live France. The second is her misfortune to die in an era that may in future be defined by its devotion to novelty. When her last work, the near perfect *A Suit of Light*, was published posthumously in 2000, some major newspapers did not even carry a review. There was an assumption that Anne Hébert had been "done". The "public", whoever they are, had moved on.

There's also the fact that Hébert's books, as far as I can determine, have been published in English (apart from the trade PaperJacks edition of *Kamouraska* occasioned by the film) "only" by the prestigious literary house of Anansi and, earlier, by the Musson Book Co.

It reflects poorly on the book industry, that publication by a literary press should work against a writer in the popular mind but it can happen. When House of Anansi published four of Hébert's novels in one volume, one major newspaper received no review copy. The kindest construction here is that such oversights have mainly to do with the marketing and distribution process, the areas that plague all small publishers trying to operate on a tight budget in this vast country. I should love to peek into an alternate, parallel reality and see how Anne Hébert was faring as an author published in translation by Harper Collins.

But any consideration of a writer's reception has ultimately to look to the work itself. Hébert's preoccupations with guilt and with the ravages of passion are themes that at first glance strike the contemporary reader as Romantic — with a great seriffed capital 'R'. All the props are in place to confirm the impression: the human heart out of control, the soul in agony, Nature anthropomorphized (unapologetically), phantasms, folklore, rural isolation, provincial suffocation, crimes of passion. Why go there when Flaubert, Brontë did it so well? For many reasons. To begin with, we have to learn to live with our unruly hearts.

Romanticism in its time acknowledged our deepest impulses, what were thought to be our most human qualities — love, hate, greed, pride, shame, joy, fear, compassion — recognizing love as the ace in the pack that won the game of the moment: union with a transcendent power. Transcendent power is now defrocked and "basic human nature" is exposed as a jumble of twitches entirely contingent on whatever (themselves contingent) values — honour, courage, beauty, cowardice — are applied as a stimulus. But we're still left with the problem of functioning with this twitchy, knee-jerking machine, like it or not. To deny the passions because they are summoned by mere constructs, is as unhelpful as disregarding (and so refusing to learn how to manage) the bodies which move our consciousness through space because they are mere products of biological processes. The passions are not to be disregarded. They are our interior lives made flesh; without them we live in isolation. No doubt we'll find all compounded in the long run, our deepest emotions the product of biochemical reaction, but no matter. They are the stuff of our lives and there is no evidence that we've ever functioned without them.

Just as you can call value-based moral choices conditioning, you can call the emotions instinct, or bio-chemical reactions, you can call them residual animal instinct, a hard-wiring for survival (Desire that strong man! Pity that helpless infant!), but you can't eradicate them. The labels peel off. The product is the same.

While our way of thinking about identity is being radically adjusted we seem to be intent on evading the question of the passions. Yet whatever consensus on identity we reach — for whatever brief span — seems to me supremely irrelevant in the face of the passions, which will surely endure. They are the unfortunate ties that bind us to the earliest recorded literature. They are still the strings that ultimately move us across this stage. And we will always need artists and writers to show us ways of being, even while the strings tug and twitch.

❖

The spring of 2003 saw the publication by Anansi of Anne Hébert's *Collected Later Novels: Burden of Dreams; Aurélien, Clara, Mademoiselle and the English Lieutenant; Am I Disturbing You?* and *A Suit of Light*, all of them translated by Sheila Fischman. (Sheila is in company with Michael Ondaatje, William Trevor and Beryl Bainbridge as one of the handful of writers to whom I've ever written fan-letters. Only Fischman and Ondaatje replied, leading me to think, like a true Canadian, "Arrogant Brits.") The English prose is so clean, its rhythms so unfaltering that the reader never once questions what the original might have been. It's our good fortune that Fischman has the expertise to preserve

Hébert's clarity of vision as well as the purity and precision of her language.

Though living as an expatriate, Anne Hébert was producing, almost to the end of her life, truly Canadian work. Even *Am I Disturbing You?*, whose narrative present is situated in Paris, is bound by its roots to rural Québec, while both *Burden of Dreams* and *Aurélien, Clara, Mademoiselle and the English Lieutenant* are saturated with the flavour of the Province. Hébert doesn't need much space to create the Québec she knew in her youth and returned to in her last years. The details are select but sharp — the grating sound of the gears of a truck, the children's boots leaving puddles on the knotty plank floor of the corner store — the brush strokes quick and masterly. "A tiny log cabin stands in a treeless field. An enormous garage with a tin roof that gleams in the light of the cold sun." But this is not the sort of nostalgia-driven writing that has enblandished (a ghastly word of my own devising that echoes how I feel after reading about yet more feisty grandmothers, rancorous fathers and batty old aunts) much of our regional literature. And it is so much more than the mimetic, documentative writing that Margaret Laurence made popular and whose hordes of imitators flattened the literary landscape for years to come with their pedestrian efforts. Hébert's world suggests vertiginous depths (routinely denied by rationalists until life has them miss their footing) beneath our own flat feet.

Her accommodation of those depths may be one of the characteristics that puts Anne Hébert's writing slightly out of step with taste today, even though she's careful to avoid any suggestion that the intangible forces she reveals owe their existence to anything other than an access of that biochemical activity her literary forbears called the passions. With the exception of the ghost tale, *Héloïse*, her work is without reference to the metaphysical or the numinous. The forces of love, jealousy, desire — whose sources are human — are strictly confined within the physical world.

It's Hébert's particular application of local detail that pulls her writing out of the purely regional descriptive mode and into the rural gothic, a convention she bends to her purpose of exploring the shadows of the psyche. Her firm hold on language keeps her material safe from melodrama. If I were to dream Hébert's prose it would be a black, fast-moving river, channelled between strong walls of glittering white concrete.

She exploited the possibilities of rural gothic in *Kamouraska*, again in *In The Shadow of The Wind*, and she's returned to it often. It surfaces again, strangely, in central Paris in *Am I Disturbing You?* The raw and the elemental erupt in the centre of the city as the two men, Stéphane and Edouard, struggle to come to terms with the presence of the crazy-sane girl they find wandering the streets. Delphine's story comes to us filtered through her own rambling narratives as received by the cool, dispassionate but profoundly disturbed (in his self-containment) Edouard.

" . . . and even the grass, along the ditches, salted with dust, is perfumed by the wind and the breathing of death and me, I've been running down the road since morning, scented by the fields and by death on the back of my neck, and Patrick drives up in his old car, his suitcase full of flies and fish hooks, and he takes me in . . . " At first glance wild and rambling, this extract, only a small part of one of Delphine's long, run-on accounts, proves, on careful inspection, to be tightly controlled. There's not a word or a punctuation mark that isn't working. The lack of a comma after the first "death" is no accident; it forces that "me" to do the job of two, introducing the next reference but also acting retrospectively to erase the border between Delphine and the landscape, now coloured and perfumed by her own experience. No accident, either, that Patrick sells fishing tackle; there's an irony to be savoured when he callously lures Delphine only to find himself for a time — long enough at least to thoroughly disturb his own affairs — on the hook.

This is a poet's work. It was as a poet that Hébert first found recognition. Her collection, *Le Tombeau des Roix*, established her territory and displayed her unique relation-ship with language that dresses extravagence of thought and feeling in classic simplicity. Even in her prose Anne Hébert saw the world through the poet's eye and described it with the poet's tongue, one of the most compelling reasons to revist Flaubert's ground. Most readers appre-ciate the rewards of his prose where '*le mot juste*' is the governing principle and the concrete detail is almost tangible. It's an additional pleasure to have such writing describe our own world: "Twisted cars. Ambulances, police and firemen, screaming sirens. Soon we'll have to take stock of the night that is ending and decide between the dead and the living, while dawn falls over the city like the silver drizzle of rain." (*A Suit of Light*)

The music of this language — and it's the simplest of languages, the plain, the pure always preferred over the complex, the ornate — is intoxicating: " . . . a muted rain has started to fall, small, widely-spaced drops, clearly perceptible but hard as pearls spilled onto the leaves and the log roof." Reading *Aurélien, Clara, Mademoiselle and the English Lieutenant* in the original, I was sixteen again and reading Verlaine. Here is more of the rain, this time in Hébert's French: *"chaque perle dure dans l'air sonore."* Music you can see!

And then there's the pleasure of story. Most writers who have the courage and vision to forge ahead on their own have done literature a service. Most of their imitators have done just the opposite. The modernists who revealed, and revelled in, the interior dramas of the mind through stream-of-consciousness spawned a welter of narrative imitations. We've all read narratives that amount to nothing more than our immobilized protagonist remembering, fretting, or yearning, short stories where nothing much at all happens either inside or outside the skull. They might be better termed stream-of-prose. Hébert restores story to the heart of narrative. In *Kamouraska* she gives us both stream-of-consciousness — in full flood — and a compelling tale.

The essence of story is that it goes somewhere. And it sweeps us with it. A working story brings to bear a certain force, like the Mariner's eye, that we're powerless to resist.

The very first sentences of *Aurélien, Clara, Mademoiselle and the English Lieutenant* announce the presence of dynamite. "It happened abruptly, in lightning fashion . . . Present, future, past, eternity — at one stroke all were abolished." The word 'eternity' enters that hyperbole with a thunder-clap. The daring is typical of Hébert. This tale is a small finely crafted gift packed with explosive. How you want to turn it in your hands, view every angle! How you continue even though you know . . . The sentences that end the earliest paragraphs leave us in no doubt that we are going on a cliff walk — near the edge: the newborn emerges "from between the thighs of her dying mother in a fountain of blood"; the child finds the words of the school teacher charged, like her flamboyant hair "with the same gilt and reddish radiance so superb one could die from it."

If I am to sit still for a tale, let me put my trust in a narrator who won't waste my time with false starts and poorly laid paths. I want a narrator who understands the strategic placement of innuendo and can intimate what is to come without turning a floodlight on the path. Let me savour the suspense and then surprise me anyway.

I like being driven forward under the illusion I'm participating, anticipating what is to come. It's one of the great satisfactions of reading. Hébert's changing tenses are the equivalent of sleight of hand. Here is the opening of the sequence in *Burden of Dreams*, where the three young people take the canoe out on the river in flood:

> "The Ouellet's canvas canoe has been freshly caulked and painted. For a long moment the red of the canoe, the yellow of Hélène's oilskin, the blue of Lydie's jacket, the red of her scarf — all these bright colours gliding along the river are visible from the shore, at high noon.
>
> When the river brought them in sight of the flat village, several recognized the red canoe and its passengers.

As she sits motionless in the canoe,
Hélène can feel with her whole body the
shock of the waves . . . "

The single words "brought" and "recognized", with their conspicuous past tenses, have the reader leaping forward in time and constructing, from her own imagination she thinks, an aftermath in which the villagers on the bank tell what they saw as the canoe passed. Imparting this thrill of anticipation to the audience is one of the oldest tools of the story teller. It's common in the folk tale and surfaces in street theatre and pantomime. ('Look behind you! Look behind you!' — a technique used and overused by popular film-makers who want to build suspense.) It's a hard trick for a writer to pull off. Telegraph too clearly and your readers will see you waving from the cliff top. They'll snap the book shut.

But this is like dissecting a living thing and likely to destroy it. Each part of Hébert's work performs not only its own allotted task but also a supporting role in the working of the whole. The poetry of Mademoiselle's red hair, for instance, in *Aurélien, Clara, Mademoiselle and the English Lieutenant* performs a double function. It makes a visual image of an intangible (the child's perception of the teacher) and simultaneously suggests a line of development. Similarly, in *Burden of Dreams*, rural Québec conjures the story's setting, creates its atmosphere and drives the narrative. Where nothing is without meaning and every detail signifies, narrative tension can be wound ever tighter. On first meeting the Englishman and being given a glass of water, the unsophisticated Clara of *Aurélien, Clara, Mademoiselle and the English Lieutenant*, having never seen ice cubes in a glass "takes pleasure in leaving the warm marks of her fingers on it."

In a climate of ideas where neither language nor things nor indeed ideas themselves can be relied on to surrender meaning, it's easy to see how this sort of writing can be undervalued. Hébert's unabashedly Romantic treatment of the natural world doesn't sit well in the present literary landscape. The woods, the river, the air alive with insects, both announce and inform the interior lives of Hébert's cast. I can't read these two apparently straightforward sentences from *Burden of Dreams* without a shiver of anticipation: "The Zoël Ouellets built their house on this steep hill shielded from the river and its heady sound, in the middle of fields lying at the end of a long lane that's hard to keep up in winter because of the snow. Three silvery poplars rustle above the house." The placement of those poplars in their short sentence announces something beyond concrete detail. Though the intent of course is not to imbue the the trees or the house with meaning but to wake us, the readers, to the nuances within the coming story itself.

Such manipulation of our response, by juxtaposition, by allusion and metaphor, to make us aware of what can be felt but not seen, belongs to the omniscient narrator, the voice of authority — long since missing, presumed dead in the literary world. But, as with any literary convention, the worst practitioners cause it to fall into disrepute; the expert uses it to produce art.

Here is the opening of a chapter from the same book. "False summer breezes, the sun beating fiercely on the brown ploughed fields. These brief flamboyant days, these bright red leaves — there is nothing in the world more beautiful, and evening is quick to return all this splendour to the deep darkness that is like a foreboding of endless winter." And the immense, dark image of the river accompanies the novel's most powerful moments. The narrative carries us with unswerving purpose on its current of human passions. In *Aurélien, Clara, Mademoiselle and the English Lieutenant,* Clara's awakened sexuality is the river that gleams and surges through the pages.

The cynical contemporary reader could easily dismiss such conventions: river equals sexuality, forest glade equals self-revelation. We're understandably weary of darkness that always signifies foreboding, storms that accompany a climax, but Hébert is afraid of nothing. She's willing to risk even the familiar, placing these notations so that they seem to grow organically from the story, making each one particular and fresh with her eye for detail. This is how the chapter opens when the fifteen-year old Clara, loud in cast-off clothes and cheap lipstick, is going to offer herself to the English lieutenant: "There is a rainbow, all its colours precise, while a second arc is forming behind the first, fragile as a glint in the water." And, should we still be resistant, Hébert neatly undermines our scepticism with irony. The Lieutenant, on seeing Clara, laughs out loud. Nothing less sentimental, more disillusioned, than this post-coital cup of tea in *Aurélien, Clara, Mademoiselle and the English Lieutenant*: "The kitchen table between them. The red and white checked oilcloth. The last package of crumbling biscuits. The boiling water poured over the last tea-leaves. The Lieutenant's provisions are exhausted." And nothing more charged.

Irony, too, is at work full-time in *Aurélien, Clara, Mademoiselle and the English Lieutenant,* where Hébert has dressed her story in the trappings of the fairy tale — and then played with some cross-dressing. The very structure of the long title announces her game and the tale itself is filled with familiar conventions: the daughter in care of the father, the house in the woods, the enchanted circle, the treasure bequeathed, the sleeping beauty, the beast,winning the heart. But it's all strangely topsy-turvy. The treasure is nothing more — and nothing less — than the lonely school mistress's rings and dresses, the heart that Clara wins is hers; the sleeping beauty is no other than the English Lieutenant in his forest hide-out suffering from pathological cowardice, fast asleep while Clara feasts her eyes on him; and Clara is the prince who comes to wake him and be woken, riding not on a white horse but on a wobbly bicycle.

In fairy tale the human and the faerie world collide. In *Aurélien, Clara, Mademoiselle and the English Lieutenant,* the poor powerless deluded humans are the figures of faerie. The English lieutenant, the soldier far from his home, is also the Green Man in the woods; Clara, the maiden, is also the brilliant, ironic, parodic fata morgana. Associated with damp earth, wild birds, strawberries, she's Maya, she's Flora. The lieutenant is "wild about her smell". She's the sprite who longs to be mortal making her journey by rickety bicycle, dressed in her schoolmistress's cast-offs, to offer herself to the beast in his lair. To set him free.

Hébert's dispassionate gaze, her lack of commentary on all this human turbulence and folly is what saves the tale from sentimentality. She learned her art from Flaubert's writing. Of that I am sure. *The Legend of St. Julian the Hospitaler* is saved from melodrama by the same means.

And so is *In The Shadow of the Wind*. There are passages in both where the writers could be interchanged. But though Hébert can match Flaubert's precise application of *le mot juste* and his effortless forward momentum, she has a more flexible use of language. That agility and an even cooler irony, as well an effortless assumption of voice, both male and female, situate her prose squarely in its own time.

It's a distinctly contemporary sensibility that has us sliding around on the untrustworthy ground of *Am I Disturbing You?* For a while we prefer to trust the rational narrative voice of Edouard, glad that we're not as gullible as his tender-hearted friend Stéphane. But then Edouard too takes liberties. He's in collusion with his creator and their voices elide to describe moments and feelings that he can't have known: Delphine's arrival at Stéphane's apartment, the intimate scene when Stéphane makes his mad proposal or even the sounds and sensations that Stéphane can hear and feel on the train out of Paris. As the narrative progresses Edouard becomes more entangled in its net. Still, "Caught in the act of listening and heeding, I refuse to follow this little girl along the uncertain roads of loss and desolation."

Like us, Edouard knows he is on slippery ground. Every reference to Delphine's story emphasizes it.

"Herself, always herself, reflected in a mirror that is itself reflected in another mirror, and so on from mirror to mirror until the head spins, while Delphine's voice dwindles away." Here is a writer as comfortable in the contemporary world of refracted surfaces and created identities as she is in the ancient landscape of the ruling passions.

Those who care to interpret literary works in the context of nationalisms (I am not among them) might find in Hébert's almost obsessive treatment of innocence and experience a representation of Canada's emergence from backwoods to city. It's more profound. Great writing, even while honouring its roots, always turns our attention to the universal. Despite the earthy, grounded details that announce Hébert's regionality, her themes never stray far from the elemental, the fundamental. *Burden of Dreams*, for example, carries with it a current of connection through the body to the earth itself, to the forces of nature; Hébert shows us our conflicting desires both to ride those forces and to transcend them, and the paradox, the deeper mystery, that we can escape them momentarily through the union of the flesh. In this slim book (just one hundred pages), Hébert makes her statement about the preservation of innocence and the winning of liberty, showing us what we consistently forget — that each carries its own price. Neither innocence without experience, nor experience that has never known innocence can constitute a human life. None of us can have one without the other.

Post-modern thought has done its best to eliminate absolute truths and we're easily persuaded of the relativity of many we once took for granted. We've succeeded handsomely in cleaning out society's lumber room of untrustworthy constructs, whether left over from old regimes or fabricated by today's power-mongers; someone had to do it and we brush the dust off our hands with satisfaction; yet in that same attic is an immoveable trunk. Perhaps it is nailed to the floor. It contains what it means to be human, the poor rags that are as close as we'll come to eternal verities. For, just as there are verities in the physical world (whose labels we may decide to change but whose hard facts are not negotiable — that the earth is a rock hurtling round the sun for instance, or that we all have blood in our veins) — so there are intangible verities. Pace Baudrillard and company, some things are actually immutable (at least in any time frame that we can relate to): the power of desire to alter the course of a life, the power of love to destroy as well as to create; they are the elementary attributes of human life — direct products not of society and its fluid discourse but of the very condition of being human. Anne Hébert is one of those who regularly unlock this trunk and display its contents for us.

❖

Few publishers would care to throw down the gauntlet to reviewers by printing the words, "A Novel" on the front cover of a book comprising 103 sparsely printed pages, but that is exactly what Anansi did when it brought out the original edition of *A Suit of Light*. It would take a small miracle for such a slip of a book to offer everything a reader asks of a novel — exactly what Anne Hébert left us. Try to describe this book and the many layers it contains, in the same amount of ink its author used, and you'll be defeated.

Played out from a modest Paris apartment block, *A Suit of Light* is the story of Miguel Almevida, son of Rose-Alba, flamboyant concierge with a voracious appetite for sexual attention, and her construction worker husband, Pedro, self-appointed guardian of peasant values and the honour of their homeland, Spain. Miguel, when the story opens is "a child who still wavers between a boy and a girl" and it's soon apparent, as he luxuriates in his mother's cosmetics and dresses, which sex he would choose were it only possible.

He's also a child with a clear eye for the truth and a wicked line in hyperbole that's perfectly tuned to the excesses of his fiery parents. Watching them through Miguel's eyes "Roaring like bulls in the ring. Rolling from one end of the tiny kitchen to the other" and leaving each other bitten and clawed is enough to make us want to cower in the broom closet with him. We quickly love him not just for the "lake of tears at his feet" but for his child's funny, solemn dignity: "My father promises to buy her another dress and a slice of steak for her eye. It's easy to see he suffers a thousand deaths . . . "

These volatile characters move so fast and with such dangerous, giant leaps towards their disparate desires that you can't afford to take your eyes off them for a second. Here (as elsewhere in her work) are no post-modern cul-de-sacs, no philosophical look-outs where you can buy time. This narrative has you by the wrist and it's heading for the precipice edge. In no time Miguel has turned fifteen, is out on the street and meeting his perverse guardian angel, Jean-Ephrem de la Tour, black, beautiful, male and dancing nightly at the Paradis Perdu. Oh, and clothed in little more than a pair of giant wings and a dazzle of lights.

It's here that Hébert's deceptively concise tale takes on mythic dimensions, for this is Lucifer in all his intelligence and beauty and outrageous self-love — and the suit of light is not the matador's costume dreamed by Pedro and Rose-Alba at all. Miguel — Michael — is us and his struggle with the dark side of beauty is ours, his story an illumination of the ruin that beauty drags in its train.

The book sweeps us from the fall of the angels to the twentieth century and the philosophical vision of Simone Weil who recognized the cruelty of beauty and the granite obduracy of grace. It's the coronation of a life's work that really began in the dark pages of *Kamouraska*, with its vision of "tragic, implacable beauty, sufficient unto itself." The same darkness is here certainly, the violence, the destructive desire. This is the human heart, after all. We can say with Miguel "I should like you not to exist," but in another millenium it — the heart — will still be with us.

Hébert's vision has, nevertheless, evolved. *Kamouraska*, despite its 1970 publication date, was still in the shadow of the nineteenth century. Guilt was the dominant motif, the monstrous oppressor of responsibility. With *A Suit of Light*, there is no guilt. There is a sense of accountability for one's own actions. There is even, from Miguel, a sense of responsibility for the other.

It's fitting that this particular book should conclude Anne Hébert's work. It's a distillation of the finest in her writing, the creation of the stylist and the visionary, her words woven into her thought's own suit of light.

In time, I believe, Anne Hébert's work will receive due recognition in English. Her work has already crossed national borders (*Kamouraska* has been translated into at least seven languages), its themes as pertinent to the French woman, the Israeli or the Thai. "Too many grown-ups in the world. Too many little girls who cross the frontier and join the cohorts of grown-ups who are huge and without pity. Only little girls with smooth bellies, asleep amid their rumpled wings, can lay claim to the sweetness of the world."

Because of its narrative drive and dramatic power, each of her novels, with the exception perhaps of *Héloïse*, has the makings of a fine film and so has the potential to reach a wider audience. But, more fundamentally, her work will endure because of its substance, illuminating as it does the darkest and most destructive of our impulses, lighting paths we'd do well not to take and speaking directly to the innate (never mind if illusory) sense of the individual that resides in each of us. I can't foresee a time when we'll tire of reading about the forces of life and death, or the corruption of innocence, or the longing for experience. Hébert's particular province brings with it a constantly renewed contemporary relevance. And the writing itself ensures its own survival, for it offers fresh rewards with each rereading.

❖

There is a translator's afterword to *A Suit of Light*. In it, Sheila Fischman writes "Anne Hébert has changed forever the way I view and interpret aspects of certain landscapes, landscapes both natural and emotional."

When I first read *Kamouraska* all that time ago, I too felt something alter in me. I began to write fiction of my own. For years, I wouldn't go near another Hébert book for fear of her influence. I wanted to find my own voice. But the spell was already cast. I wrote my first novel, *The Blackbird's Song*, heavily under the influence, as it were. It was only after reading *A Suit of Light*, more than twenty years later, that I found the courage to brave Anne Hébert's other books. And I re-read *Kamouraska*. I could see at once what my book had taken from her, the stifling atmosphere of passion suppressed, repressed, the violence. I only wish I had seen all this in time to write to Anne Hébert and acknowledge the debt. I'm still learning from her.

THE THIN RED LINE TO THE IMMANENT

IN AN ATTEMPT TO COME TO TERMS with the philosophical problem of affliction, I had been reading Simone Weil and the Spanish philosopher Miguel de Unamuno. Both locate affliction centrally in their individual vision of God. I tried several times to engage with Unamuno. In his best known work, *The Tragic Sense of Life*, he makes some difficult categorical statements about war and God and the necessity of war as an expression of God. I put him aside. Months later, a rented Hollywood video, Terrence Malick's *The Thin Red Line*, helped me to understand some of these prickly ideas, if only on an instinctual, intuitive level. Here was a meditation on war that I could relate to: no difficult statements here, no shocking assertions about war being the supreme vehicle for the expression of God, only questions. *The Thin Red Line* is riddled with questions, though the connotations of that phrase — machine gun fire, rapidity, noise and senseless destruction — are entirely at odds with the stillness at the heart of the film. Its questions are formulated slowly, asked with deep perplexity and an aching sense of something withheld, hidden. This is how it feels to be stumbling about in a world where good and evil coexist.

It was a kind of ambush, this movie. During my childhood and early teen years in England, war films, in black and white, were standard Sunday night entertainment on television. These were the films about World War II: resourceful British soldiers, brave Yanks, hateful Nazis, courageous resistance fighters and commando units. I enjoyed the gut-wrenching and the nail-biting, the challenge of being first to spot the traitor or the coward. Enjoyment was wholehearted and unadulterated and I was entitled to it, born into a nation of victors — not any old victors but victors in a cause the world unanimously acknowledged as just. Monday night documentaries were all the evidence I needed. This was the post war period when new footage, salvaged from Nazi concentration camps was continually being released. Sometimes this footage, shot within the camps, would be included in the nightly news, more often it would be compiled in documentary format. Am I imagining that it would be preceded by a warning to "those of a nervous disposition" not to watch? I watched every second with sick fascination and knew myself to be changed by what I saw. There is nothing as existential as horror. Nothing as irrefutable, as indissoluble. No objection to any amount or degree of violence perpetrated by Allied troops could stand in light of these documentaries; there was no question that the war had to be fought. Bombing and shelling didn't begin to weigh in the balance against bodies of naked men, women and children piled like carcasses at an abattoir. I was smugly grateful to find myself on the good team, whose players were all aglitter with honour and self-sacrifice, valour, courage and glory. But there were more documentaries to come and the BBC, before too long, was showing more footage, this time film of the aftermath of Hiroshima and Nagasaki. Crimes against humanity were no longer exclusive to Nazi Germany. The problem seemed to be the impulse to violence *per se*, which was everywhere granted tenure through state-sanctioned militarism.

It's likely that the pacifist movement in England gained much of its momentum from the impact of the graphic documentation of violence that entered our living rooms in the late fifties and early sixties. My appetite for war films waned. They were insidious: manipulative in their selectivity, remiss in their omissions. I turned instead to the War poets and found in them the confirmation I was looking for. It's *all* a myth, the whole shebang. There is *no such thing* as this abstract called collectively honour and glory. Somebody has to make it up. Other people have to go off and fight for it.

Most film on war, even if it purports to be anti-war, is heavily flavoured with honour and glory, preparing the palate to accept the killing of some people some of the time and concealing the rottenness inherent in the principle of armed conflict. Acutely aware of having been duped into my own share of flag waving and blind allegiance, I was finished with war movies.

Still from time to time they turn up, and here was one brought home from the video store and I was curled on the couch and all of the preceeding is by way explaining why I was taken so unaware. I had not expected to stay awake much past the time it took to finish my coffee. But, ambushed by Terrence Malick's art, I was held captive and compelled to watch, transfixed by his rendering of the human condition and his contemplation of its meaning. A slow Kentucky voice asked the question, "What is this war in the heart of nature?" Zoroastrianism? In a twentieth century combat zone? The men on the screen were picking their way, silently, through dense jungle. The voice over, belonging to the film's Private Witt, continued, "Not one power but two?" Manicheism? What was this? Hollywood not only acknowledging the numinous but toying with dualism? *The Thin Red Line* was marching straight across cliché-pocked terrain (the small band of men, acquitting themselves, against impossible odds, with honour, decency and courage) into a denser jungle beyond with its tangle of riddles and paradox springing from a single root. Through the beautiful meditations that permeate the work (and poetry was something else I did not expect), the film looks unflinchingly at the most difficult and important questions of human existence: what is this place where we find ourselves? Who are we and what is it that connects us? What is this Immanence that we sense through the beauty of the world and why can't we touch it? The film looks at immortality, the mystery of life and death and its connectedness, the mystery of our connectedness to one another and the possibility of our connectedness with an Immanence. To contemplate these things, Malick uses a language that has the simplicity, clarity, and directness of poetry — the only language tough enough to grasp paradox without falling apart — and a camera eye that displays for us the unbearable loveliness and cruelty of creation.

For the sake of readers who might not have seen the film, the outline is simple: a company of American soldiers is deposited during World War II on strategically important Guadalcanal and ordered to take a Japanese stronghold. They achieve their objective. The survivors leave. This story is played out in a strange and beautiful setting where

Malick has both Nature and the Melanesians who live on Guadalcanal remain aloof and impervious to the carnage.

The film opens with the image of a crocodile — death and destruction easing itself into the heart of Nature the serpent in the garden — but follows at once with a long and loving look at a world filled with grace and beauty: the Solomon islanders living (for Malick's purpose) harmoniously in a setting of Tropical loveliness representing the possibility of Paradise, the beauty of creation, the world as it might have been, as we wish it to be. The lyrical imagery of Nature is more than a backdrop; it gives *The Thin Red Line* its power and its depth and is central to Malick's view; it is the Nature of Rumi, of Francis of Assisi, of Eckhart, of Spinoza; it is, it might be, Brahman. One of the most compelling sequences, set in deep forest early in the film, is one where nothing happens. The soldiers are walking in stillness. It is a stillness so intense and awful that it is a presence and they are not before it but within it. And this of course is the pantheism that has been resisted by Judeo-Christian philosophers but that has flowed anyway into the works of the mystics. It's the pantheism that permeates Hinduism. In fact the meditation that occurs in voice-over at this point in the film, "You're death that captures all. You, too, are the source . . . " is a clear and beautiful echo of the Upanishads.

The film's most affective moment comes during its most harrowing sequence, a protracted and graphic depiction of close combat. It's the familiar horrors-of-war scene, but where other directors would have us firmly on the side of the men whose fortunes we've been following, Malick has us instead crying "No," at their very moment of victory; when we weep we are weeping for "the enemy" who are falling like animals, falling as we would, under fire and under the knife. We weep for ourselves. There is no overestimating Terrence Malick's achievement here. He tells us nothing. Instead, he sets us down within the scene and makes us feel, makes us know the truth his characters grope towards. We are all one — but not in any sentimental or consoling sense; we are all implicated in the terrible web of Creation and no amount of idealism can save us. "Do you imagine your sufferings will be less because you loved goodness, truth?" asks the dead face of the enemy. The camera's lingering close-up serves the same purpose as the Renaissance *Memento Mori*: "As you are now, so once was I; as I am now, so too will you be." It's also cold and stingingly ironic confirmation of the inkling that had come to the Kentucky soldier early in the film: "Maybe all men got one big soul everybody's a part of . . . " In striking out at another we wound ourselves.

In the weeks preceding Rembrance Day, 2001, a short-lived but animated discussion sprang up in the local media about the most edifying contemporary war film to watch in — I'm sure someone must have said it — "these troubled times." *Saving Private Ryan* was championed by most, on the grounds, I suspected, of the number of Oscars for which it was nominated and or won. *Apocalypse Now* was high on the list as was *Platoon* and *Schindler's List*. I don't remember *The Killing Fields* being cited and no one at all mentioned *The Thin Red Line*. I began to haunt the video store.

It was obvious that *Saving Private Ryan*'s reputation as an anti-war statement was spuriously earned and rested solely on the ferocious carnage of the film's opening sequence (the Allied landing under heavy fire on Omaha beach). The rest of the film belongs squarely with the war films of the 1950s and early '60s, ending with a ridiculously unlikely shoot-out designed to warm the cockles of young males everywhere. Only extras get minced to mash by gunfire, the real cast, you and I, survive, get a fetchingly placed wound, or die a hero to the accompaniment of music that suggests the experience must be something akin to a fabulous orgasm. *Schindler's List*, a film with a similarly high reputation is fatally marred by a similarly daft ending, this one somehow managing to discount millions of everyday acts of courage and sacrifice and even, it seems, the Jews themselves beside the super-elevated portrayal of Schindler. (Am I mistaken in thinking that in the final turgid scene all of the extras crowding Schindler were at least head and shoulders shorter than him?)

My search for a recent film to match *The Thin Red Line* was unsuccessful. *The Killing Fields* comes close. It's a disturbing film to watch and its treatment of war is uncompromising but its focus on the individual story of survival keeps it just short of universality. Francis Ford Coppola's *Apocalypse Now*, generally acknowledged as a masterpiece of its kind, carries undeniable heft, yet something — is it Coppola's presence, the visible brush strokes on the painting? — makes it less accessible, less approachable. It remains the director's awesome creature and seems barely to pertain to us at all.

Full Metal Jacket, an astute satire on the militarization of men, illustrates the difficulty inherent in making anti-war statements through film. Kubrick shaves his point so fine here that I suspect the film has been viewed, and enjoyed, widely as an action picture. The abscence of an identifiable mission, the total lack of coherence or relevance of the action in the already destroyed city is likely seen as a short-coming rather than a central point, if it is noticed at all. The final scene, that has the soldiers silhouetted against a symbolic sunset, indistinguishable one from the other, deliv-ering in male voice choir perfection as they march the chant M-I-C-K-E-Y-M-O-U-S-E, deftly throws the responsibility for tribalism back into the lap of the audience, that is, society itself — but I doubt that the people who watch for the gore factor would feel a thing. *Das Boot* also makes its point through the very shape of the film itself. It can be watched as high adventure — the band of men against all odds, the test of courage and endurance — until the final sequence when the intense focus pulls back to offer a panoramic vision of blind destruction. Not even the finest qualities — hope, courage, faith, love — can save us. A quotation embedded in the heart of this film touches on our deadly desire to break the bounds of the merely human and find the absolute. "To be heading into the inexorable, where no mother will care for us, where no woman crosses our path, where only reality reigns with cruelty and with grandeur." The path of danger is a potential route, although most of us stumble at the first steps and fall readily into abject, disgracing fear. The irony, inherent in the film's overarching metaphor, is that the absolute, the inexorable contains our destruction within it. The quotation inciden-tally could also put a valid construction on our fascination with violence in film, though the majority who indulge it are merely lapping at puddles of blood. The appetite for blood and the appetite for fulfilment are at a primitive level closely related. For the most part we keep them carefully separated. When the dividing wall crumbles under pressure we get individual or group psychosis with their corresponding outcomes, murder or war.

Platoon, although set in a different war from *The Thin Red Line*, is closest to Malick's film in material and treatment and, for me, made the most interesting comparison. For a while I thought I was about to view the original from which the later film is derived. Here was the same unsettling trek through jungle, shots of sun through forest canopy, lizards doing their splayed walk, snakes coiling, decomposing bodies, the forces of life and death in juxtaposition. Here was the voice over. Oliver Stone it seemed had got there first.

His film, though, remains earthbound; Stone never leaves the side of the screen. There are many fine shots and whole sequences that could speak for themselves; instead we're treated to overt commentary in musings, in the clumsy convention of letters home and in sermonizing between characters. There's no doubt that the film has a strong moral impulse — Stone's own attempt to "find a goodness and a meaning to this life" — but its foundations are weakened, it seems to me, by capitulation to the conventional drama — black hat/white hat — that we can't seem to shake. The village massacre scene, for instance, would have only gained in power by playing it with no heroes. In the end his film is derailed by a conflict between the characters Elias and Barnes. The orchestra that accompanies Elias's agonizing death suggests that yes indeed he is going to heaven to smoke dope for all eternity. Stone pushes the morality even further and has his protagonist

Chris kill Barnes. All the scores are even. The response to violence in a successful anti-war film, on the other hand, will be sense of loss, not justice.

The Thin Red Line goes further. It is without question a deeply religious film. There are the conspicuous allusions to Eden in the shots of Melanesian life, the graphic representations of a fall from grace in the demeaning brutality of the soldiers. There is the inadequacy of institutionalised faith that leads one soldier to conclude, "We're dirt, we're just dirt." There is the existentialism of Welsh, "In this world a man himself is nothing, and there ain't no world but this one", and there is Bell's idealistic insistence on the liberating power of love. But Welsh, as the camera shows us, is wilfully blind and Bell is living an illusion. Only Private Witt's questions achieve perfect accord with their context. They are delivered quietly as the horror unfolds and this is the clue to Witt's, and I suspect, Malick's, Stoic vision. Early in the film, Witt, remembering his mother's death, says, "I just hope I can meet it with the same calm because that's where it's hidden, the immortality I hadn't seen."

The Thin Red Line is charged with electrifying questions, from Witt's first suspicions, "Who are you who live in all these many forms?" through the most difficult question at the heart of the film, "This great evil," — and I'm tempted to use capitals — "where'd it come from?" to his final words, which take the form of a prayer. It's a film with spiritual links that run from the Stoics to, in this century, Simone Weil. The French philosopher, considered the same questions: the implacable quality of Nature, the lack of finality, that is, intentionality, of beauty ("The sea is not less beautiful in our eyes because we know that sometimes ships are wrecked"), our yearning for a response, for some sign of purpose from the Universe. With the same steady eye, Weil contemplated affliction, recognizing how, in its absence of purpose or finality, affliction reveals God.

Of course Malick's steadfast gaze on evil has the undeniable advantage of fine cinematography to light it. But it is in service of the same vision. The crocodile at the end of the film is Nature brought down and defiled by man but it is also, for want of a better word, God, nailed. The image of Nature bound and degraded echoes the terrible desecration of the earlier, murderous military victory; destroy the 'enemy' and you destroy yourself. We are all part of all of It and It is part of us; we avoid ruin only by calm acceptance.

The most beautiful and enigmatic of the meditations ends the film with a haunting echo of Johann Eckhart's "The eye by which I see God is the same as the eye by which God sees me". No more questions now for Witt but a hymn of desire "O my soul let me be in you now. Look out through my eyes . . . at the things you made . . . ", words that in their mysterious syntax might have been penned by Eckhart or by the "God-intoxicated" Spinoza himself, words that strangely conflate creator and created, "features of the same face".

THE DYNAMIC OF TRUTH

ALL QUIET ON THE WESTERN FRONT, Erich Maria Remarque's novel of the Great War, is the classic slim classic and an easy read. When I first picked it up only two or three years ago I couldn't imagine how it had eluded me for so long (though I do remember ducking out of Remembrance Day observances at school and so managing to miss the film numerous times). The book bears reading and rereading.

"The classic war novel of all time" declares the jacket copy of my battered paperback. Yet it barely qualifies as a novel. It's a fictional account, simple and moving and told with composure. It's not short of graphic descriptions; Remarque pulls us into the din and the heat of ferocious shelling, the panicked terror of hand-to-hand combat. But there is a calculated measure underlying his telling, a clear-eyed vision. The book's stance is that of the veteran who sits a long time staring into his glass before he begins to speak. Then he tells you everything and there's no need for him to embellish his tale for effect. The details speak for themselves. The book's quiet manner is the restraint of profound grief. This is not the calm of resignation or the quiet of resolution, not the stillness following peace or forgiveness; this is the steady, hopeless voice of bitter loss, acute pain. It's the voice of desolation.

Set against the bulk of the nineteenth century's *War and Peace, All Quiet On The Western Front* is matchwood.

Remarque's characters are only perfunctorily sketched in; they are never more than caricatures or types. It's easy to imagine their creator sitting on an upturned box in the camp behind the lines with a sketch book on his knee; he's watching his fellow soldiers going about their duties or resting and he catches each one on the page in a gesture true to his type: the bully, the joker, the racketeer, the faithful friend. We see them in action but there are few surprises and no development. There cannot be. Remarque's business is more urgent than character study. His purpose is to show how the machine of war maims even those who survive it.

His story receives similar treatment. With no plot to speak of, *All Quiet On The Western Front* is a simple string of episodes: a soldier's experiences as he trains for, travels to and serves at the front. Like the soldiers' lives that alternate, as the narrator Paul Bäumer says, between billets and the front, Remarque's story is a succession of light and dark: travelling in convoy, going up the line on wiring fatigue, visiting the girls in the village, enduring a bombardment in no man's land; there's a revenge exacted on a sadistic sergeant, a shelling in the trenches, the arrival of raw recruits, the rescue of a comrade. Paul is wounded; his body is mended; he is returned to the front. The dynamics of a novel are missing; there is no organic growth or development here. The narrative, like the war itself, is all consuming — there is no eluding it, no deviation from its path. You know that Remarque had his list of "Must Include" passages at his elbow. Strangely, that's his strength. The dynamics of the novel have been replaced by the dynamics of life, burning need. Remarque had to write this book or be consumed by his experience.

That there is no plot (at a time when plot was central to the novel) is significant. Plot as E. M. Forster has it, is the "why?" of the thing. Narrative tells us what happened and when. Plot tells us why. Perhaps a true war novel, especially an anti-war novel, *can* have no plot. A sense of the inexorable is central to the book's magnetism and strength; developing a tale full of surprises to both writer and reader would have diluted that sense. There is no plot in war, nothing to explain the stupefying illogic of its cause or the blind savagery of its effect. The machine must roll. Remarque's war, cheered on by the rhetoric of thousands of Kantorek's (Paul's schoolmaster, who represents those who should know better), consumes the thousands more who fuel it, the Bäumers, Tjadens, Katczinskys of the fighting units, who, once it has begun to move, have no choice in the matter. When there is no choice, questions are irrelevant. "Why?" is not the word that springs to the lips of the man in a shell-hole pulling a corpse onto himself for cover. There is only what to do next. "And now . . . and now . . . "

In a passage three-quarters of the way through the book, Paul has become separated from a reconnaissance patrol and waits out the night alone and disoriented in a shell hole while a heavy bombardment from both sides is underway. When at dawn a French soldier stumbles into the same shell hole, Bäumer does not think twice. "I make no decision — I strike madly home." Unable to strike again yet equally unable to escape through the heavy fire, he waits out the remainder of the day with the dying man, at first in terror and then — when the French soldier nears his end — filled with pity and remorse. The scene culminates in a passage, addressed to the corpse, beginning "Comrade,

I did not want to kill you". "Comrade"! Bäumer makes a hasty promise to write to the man's wife. He searches the body for identification, finds letters and snapshots. He fantasizes that he will send money. But the narrative, even though it is describing a kind of madness, remains clear-eyed: "I must do everything, promise everything in order to save myself." In his heart Bäumer knows he is only bartering with God, trying to buy himself out of his predicament. Later when he makes a dash for safety he babbles that he will fulfill all the promises he has made to the corpse, "but already I know that I shall not do so."

A novel — by, say, Sebastian Faulks or David Guterson, perhaps Anne Michaels or David Adams Richards, almost certainly Jane Urqhart — would have developed the incident. I can see it as central to a more full-fledged novel: the decision to write the letter or not, the moral dilemma, the fateful consequences. Hollywood would have gone further; Bäumer would have been face to face with the widow in no time, the foot of a bed stage right. But *All Quiet On The Western Front* is neither Hollywood drama nor novel. The incident in the shell hole is just another bead on the wire. As this account gets strung together, incident follows incident, piling destruction for the protagonists, who are powerless to alter the course of events, their own actions being determined not by moral choice but the events themselves. Even heroism — as one of the final episodes shows — is meaningless. This last passage, when Bäumer's friend Katczinsky is wounded, has been filched by just about every war movie ever made. It's played various ways, always with the same outcome. But Remarque eschews facile statements about the redemptive nature of honour or courage, the transcendence of the human spirit. He leaves us where war leaves us — with bitter loss.

This is not a book that could have been written any other way. To include moral choices — that is, to turn it into a classic twentieth century novel — would have diluted its central message: war strips us of choice, the very essence of our humanity. The narrator is a cog in the war machine and knows it.

It's interesting to see what happens when a novelist from our own time and culture, Timothy Findley, uses the same theatre of war as a setting for a novel that turns on moral choice. How I should love *The Wars* to have been able to achieve in original English what *All Quiet On The Western Front* achieves, for me at least, in its translation from the German. But Findley has sabotaged his own tale. Though it has all the makings, initially, of another powerful, simple representation of war, in the end Findley's choice of material reduces its stature (or increases it, depending on what you ask of the book and on which way you view the spectrum that leads from the individual to the general). It can't do otherwise. It is the fate of any novel of war that chooses the particular over the universal. As soon as a book is weighted with details that pertain to a single character and could be assigned to no other, its gravity is undermined, its reach curtailed. We find ourselves weeping for the protagonist when we should be weeping for humanity.

The Wars, like *All Quiet On The Western Front*, follows the fortunes of a single soldier, in this case one Robert Ross. But where Remarque's narrative is picaresque, simply flinging his protagonist Paul into the war, jerking him back on leave, throwing him back in and so on, Findley's weaves a tale, and a strong one. A tough narrative thread in *The Wars* draws all events to a single point, Robert's crazy-sane act of defiance against the lunacy raging all around. It's a strong concept and though it's not without flaws it is executed extremely well — and that's the whole problem. *The Wars* is a novel of Robert Ross. Findley's material, fine as it is, works against itself. Several of the scenes of action at the front (crossing the corpse-strewn marsh in eerie fog, walking the trench clogged with the dead and wounded, and the gas attack during the gun placement) are utterly gripping, the equal of anything in Remarque. They can stand by themselves and, for them to have real significance or to make any kind of statement about war they should be allowed to. To embed them in a tale of mad heroism seems to tamper with their integrity. Any of the incidents might have happened to any soldier at the front. But the weight given to Ross's actions — that is, a whole book — falsely alters the balance of what is important here. It's as if in a painting of twenty men getting slaughtered, only one — who is, say, saving a bird — is in the foreground. (Actually, if such a painting were to exist it would be working on a purely symbolic level and would therefore have a chance make a large statement about war and the human spirit; but let's say the painter then added specifics about the soldier — placed a letter, say, with a clear address in his hand, scattered some photographs, a scarf, identifiable, nameable flowers at his feet — we should find our attention diverted to the individual story.) I'm not trying to set up here some kind of literary hierarchy where the symbolic statement outranks the individual story; I'm simply trying to explain why Findley's novel occupies a spot in literature distinct from Remarque's and performs a different function; why, should we want our own fictional classic on war, we shall still have to write it.

Beside Remarque's, Findley's work is busy. He gives us a narrative split between home and away; he nests it within a story of discovery, splitting it still further between now and then. He loads his protagonist with formative memory, has other characters puzzling over his (Robert's) and each other's motivations. He throws in an alcoholic mother, a shadowy disabled sister, a beautiful British aristocrat, her story told, through her sister's eyes, both young and old. If this had really been a novel about a group of people and the way they behaved or misbehaved, with the war as a backdrop, all would have been very well; but it isn't; it's a novel about Robert Ross in the war, in the eye of the hurricane; badly behaved socialites et al are just annoying distractions the novel can do without. Once the novelist has focused our attention on war, all other concerns are bound to seem trivial.

As well, Findley toys with his images and when he does I can almost see him at his desk greeting a recurring image, taking it in his hands and turning it to set it down again for us in a new and more revealing light. He does this for example with the avian images as well as with the images of caged animals. But this is what novelists do, you might respond. Exactly — but we must not see them doing it.

The twentieth century's stock of novels and films about both World Wars is heavy with material showing the ability of the human spirit to transcend unimaginable adversity and pain and affirm its own dignity. But perhaps it is this kind of material, seen again and again, that subtly abets the war-mongers, that keeps us all from taking to the streets.

Doris Lessing in her 1985 Massey lecture, "Prisons We Choose to Live Inside", made reference to scientific studies that had established our acute susceptibility to brainwashing of all kinds. All of us. No one, she pointed out, is blessed with immunity. In that light, softening the edges of depictions of war, vaselining the lense with a blur of redemption, starts to look decidedly pernicious. There really is nothing life affirming or redemptive about mutilation and death. The picture on the front of the newspaper that shows a grieving Bosnian/Palestinian/Iraqi mother, hands raised to the sky, mouth dragged open to release her loss, shows us, ah, yes, the extremes of human love, the feelings we know we all possess if only we could access them; it shows us nothing of the destruction and waste she bewails, the horror she has witnessed. What if her son's face were on the front page in close up, ears, nose and lips cut off because he would not rape her? Not too many warm feelings of compassion from that one. Or look on the internet instead of watching *Black Hawk Down*. It isn't too hard to find uncensored war photographs; only there won't be any rousing music as you near the end of a sequence, no shots of surviving soldiers running together, banded, bonded, exhausted but still virile, still triumphant, still human.

It was a disappointment to me when Timothy Findley having taken his protagonist to the limits of despair, turned on the music, the lyrical strings — if only for a few lines — affirming Robert Ross's spirit, his memory, his life. Findley had come so close to achieving the steadfast vision necessary for a treatment of war.

Pointing to shortcomings in a book as fine as *The Wars* seems like a vaguely mean act; it's like pointing out a glitch in an athlete's performance when he's won a silver medal. The truth is — again — that the choice of material creates an almost insurmountable problem. How to show mass slaughter and still to make each individual death count. Remarque's solution was to stick to facts, to recount each separate, each individual incident clearly, to eschew the broad, general description and to let the slow accumulation of detail build to a cohesive damning whole. No one escaped Remarque's war, especially not the survivors.

What is it then, that can make a bald account of experience into the work of art that is *All Quiet On The Western Front*? Like other "slim classics" (*A Christmas Carol, Animal Farm, The Handmaid's Tale*) the book is a distillation of all its author had to say about its subject — in this case the atrocity of war and its crime against the promise of youth. But it's precisely because of this distillation, this compression, that the book brims with emotion. There's a powerful tension at work here between Remarque's clear-eyed, clinical, observation and the kind of raw emotion that unmans. He'll have you inspect the changes wrought in a soldier's face by death, and then turn round and invite you to share the saving comfort of the voices of his friends within the circle of terror and destruction, "more to me than life . . . I could bury my face in them, in these voices . . . "

Remarque was a poet. It shows even in translation. That his language is unadorned doesn't mean it is innocent of intention. Each description has its emotional target. The wounded horses, for example, wandering the battlefield are at first made out by the men only dimly as "black clumps moving about" and then seen through binoculars in all their agony, tangling in their own guts. Even here the steady tone and clear vision hold. "And these are not men," Remarque says, "only horses." The simplest, plainest words ordered with precision carry the force of poetry.

His lyrical passages carry equal power: the descriptions of the birch woods of his home, the memory of his friend's hair "flying in his face like silk", and the one I find most moving, his visit home. The preparation for this passage is beautifully understated. His train travels through the countryside taking him, past meadow and woodland, past dark lines of swaying poplars "fashioned out of shadow, light, and desire", taking him home. Why do passages like this work where Findley's only irritate? Because they're not distracting us from the main story — Paul's progress through the war; they are part of it. He never asks us, as Findley does, to become involved in family or friends; those lives exist outside the war both for Paul and for us; they don't belong; we can let them slip by — as Paul does. Detached, they achieve the power of symbol — this is every family, every mother — and intensify our identification with Paul. He sees the names that mark the boundaries of his youth and he cannot tear himself away from the train window. The sight of the grey streets of the town affects him "as though it were my mother." But when he reaches his house his own emotions defeat him and he's unable to climb the stairs. He can only stand and lean against the wall, miserable and paralysed while the tears run down his cheeks. More than just a tug on our heart-strings, this is a metaphor for a lost generation. The longed-for homecoming is a bitter disappointment. The narrator, Paul, has been horribly refashioned by experience and the distance between him and those who love him is unbridgeable. What if our own mothers were lost to us this way? We can't say that of Ross's alcoholic mother, she's too particular, too delineated; too bad he had a mother like that, is the best we can manage.

There is much in *All Quiet On The Western Front* that we've seen a hundred times at the movies: the raw recruit who runs out from cover at the height of the shelling, the wounded comrade rescued at tremendous cost only to be pronounced dead on arrival. There are the blueprints here for at least a dozen scenes. To read them in their original form, in Remarque's clear prose is to see them for the first time in all their power. For the most part the work that we are used to, the work that has been modelled on them, suffers from a fatal weakness. In nearly every case it has been adulterated by our damaging need to affirm. The bleak message won't do. I'd like to know who decreed this and which planet he inhabits. I'd also like to know, were such a thing measurable, how much damage has been done to us over the last long terrible century by this diet of affirmation and optimism in connection with such a deadly compulsion. If I were the victim of a land mine or worse, I'd take no comfort from the fatuous messages of literature and film: good can come of ill, goodness can triumph over evil, the human spirit can transcend adversity. To show the atrocities of war and then to ease them with a full orchestra, an implied triumph — repeatedly — must have some effect on our consciousness similar to the magic drawing pad of the toy shop: scribble all over it, as much as you please, and then lift the top sheet. *Voilà! Rien!* All gone. You can be as bad as you like and good will always triumph. You'll still have a clean sheet. Remarque knew better. All victims of war — and the term of course includes all soldiers throughout the world — know better. To say otherwise, to soften the bleak message is to betray them. Not only that, it sets us up for another fall. The more we hear the message that the effects of war may be overcome by loyalty, courage and hope, the more we are likely to believe it. A more useful message, especially for our children, is that war is a filthy mess and a waste of lives and no one — no one — can escape its harm.

Remarque wrote two sentences as a preface to his book. "This book," he says, "is to be neither an accusation nor a confession, least of all an adventure, for death is not an adventure to those who stand face to face with it. It will try simply to tell of a generation of men who, even though they may have escaped its shells were destroyed by the war."

CONSTANCY

IN 1996 A SNOW FELL ON THE SAANICH PENINSULA on Vancouver Island, the like of which had no match in living memory. It is still talked about. Displays of meteorological force in this benign corner of Canada are rare. High winds will sometimes barrel in from the Pacific. Once, they joined with a freak tide, leaving the coastline strewn with wreckage. But in this community where the gentle climate encourages market gardens and nurseries, the wet, west coast snow of '96 let loose its own brand of destruction bringing down trees and power lines, crushing roofs and demolishing acres of greenhouses and farm buildings. All roads were impassable and twentieth century life as we knew it was suspended, holding us all in a cocoon of elemental, antique stillness.

Snow of this kind is an extravagant wonder, an unexpected gift. To wake to this new/old world was to have one's sense of astonishment renewed. It was the stuff of fairy tale. As I write this, I'm acutely consciousness of readers who have a lifetime of such snows and their attendant inconveniences behind them. For me, raised in England and living now on Vancouver Island, snow has been at best a once or twice a year occurrence, usually a mean sprinkling that barely conceals the surface of things and seldom lasts more than a week. My affair with domestic snow had been an optimist's progress of scrapey toboggan runs, and lunatic cross-country ski attempts over a smear of sticky cake decoration; heavier falls only meant boots soaking through in minutes; by afternoon the snow outside was often melting as fast as the dirty ice-clumps off the mittens by the fire.

Unless you must go out to reach your animals, or visit a sick relative, make a journey, or risk losing a week's business or wages, big snow, to those unused to it, is a kind of transubstantiation. It's the materialization of grace. It fills the house with light, raises the surface of the planet by three feet and plants picture book clouds where your shrubs and apple trees used to grow. It bestows the blessing of delight. You look in amazement on a world where definition has been erased, borders obliterated. Is that the fence post over there, that vague, box-shaped bump on top of the snow? Because you never did put the chairs away after the Indian summer, the space where the lawn used to be is now the upper surface of the planet's cloud cover seen from a plane. Whiteness, thick whiteness, thick, blankety, warm, inviting whiteness everywhere. Dumb, numb, insensate whiteness that yet wakes the senses. Ungraspable, larger than life whiteness. It is both absence and abundance. Not a single colour to be seen but its own magnificent purity, filling space, filling vision, filling the mind.

But how to get into it? How to get out of the house? There is a small space under the eaves where you can stand in the open doorway and survey the solidity of the hip-high snow — a small space where you can stand and begin shovelling. But this is the west coast; and the shovels are somewhere out there in the shed . . .

The snow's dual quality, the sense of nothing and at the same time a great deal of something, can be detected, too, by the ear. Silence is not an absence but a presence in this new environment; it confers isolation. An abundance of isolation. The power lines are down, the telephone line too. In the house there is not even the hum of the fridge. Outside, the silence is even thicker.

Your busy neighbours who love to saw things up and chop things down and give their yards the occasional blow job have disappeared; cars, even distant ones, have vanished; today there is no boat on the water, no plane in the sky. You hear a dog bark once, twice.

Isolation is part of the snow's gift. It's free entry to the refuge of hermits and mystics who know that in solitude lies deep connection with the essence of things. Whether or not "things" — trees, stones, the planet, a piece of cordwood — have an essence is almost, for me, a moot point. What is more important to me, what matters to me is that I know that there is an interior space I can reach where they *seem* to. I like it there.

Jack Hitt, the American writer, observing the parallels between environmentalism and religion, has noted that to those who care at all for the planet, environmental corruption feels like sin. I agree. And snow is absolution. It creates a new, untouched, uncontaminated world, an invitation to start over. Both blinding and revelatory, it obliterates our mistakes and our wilful damage, lays down perfect purity over our sins. And it does not do (or perhaps it does) to observe too closely how one's every action degrades it. We leave footprints.

Besides, our renewed awe at the sacredness of the material world belongs only to our immediate apprehension. The apparent splendour of this particular snowfall quickly revealed its destructive power, the wreckage beneath the immaculate loveliness. To experience snow of this kind was to come face to face, however briefly with a force of nature. It had the elemental power of wind, sun, sea. It belonged with flood, drought, fire and we were thrown back to a time when the accepted wisdom was not that we could manage nature but that we were helpless before her. The world closed in. It narrowed its orbit, leaving some of the most important furniture of our lives — electricity, the car, the bike, the telephone — outside (in the shed, as it were) and destroying others — trees, buildings — completely. For a short and, to me at least, blissful time we engaged with this event barehanded, not only measuring it against ourselves ("It's up to my hips.") but measuring ourselves against it. It was several days before the snowfall began to be measured in lost dollars and earn itself a promotion to catastrophe. In the process it began to lose its immediacy — as if the real event had happened elsewhere, where a collapsed marina had sunk millions of dollars-worth of boats, where a huge greenhouse operation would now face bankruptcy. There were no economic consequences for my family. Did that mean that "our" snow was only a miraculous dream, all that dazzle, that extravagant gesture from heaven, that piling of the world with light, that mind-bending spin on soft and firm, heavy and light, wet and dry, that wealth?

Mediated events can be observed, celebrated, wept over and then, in an anomalous vindication of the Buddhist view of the emotions, put aside in favour of the daily round; this event imposed real change. We organized ourselves to make sense of the new environment, living by oil lamps and wood heat and reverting, happily at first, to an earlier time. How easy then to see the virtue of co-operation over competition. Interesting too to note how our system of measurement regressed in relation to the snow: at first a few centimetres, then two feet, and finally waist high — the body in direct contact with the elements. In the evening we ate together, played cards by candlelight, brought out the guitar — though it was not hard to look a week down the road and see frayed tempers and strained relationships, the sudden warmth flaring into cabin fever.

It took three days of intermittent lackadaisical shovelling to reach the road. The work began in a frenzy but lost its thrust as the truth of the matter dawned: the drive is more than 100 metres long; at the end of it there would be nowhere to go. The news clips we are used to viewing each winter show east coasters shovelling hip-high snow from their front paths — in front of camera crews who have travelled along freshly ploughed roads to film them. No one would be sending a rare west-coast snow plough down our long and sparsely built road. On day two, the sons were dispatched to confirm the theory. After almost an hour of wading, they returned. There was no urgency. We settled in to savour the paradox: absence and presence, deprivation and abundance, all and nothing.

The road at the end of the driveway runs in a straight line for one kilometre until it meets the main road. It's wide enough for the recycling truck to pass a delivery van if both slow down and hug the shoulder. On one side, for the whole length, a wide grass boulevard separates the road from a dark wall of tall hemlock and Douglas fir, broken only where the gravel or dirt driveways cut out to the road; on the other side the same width of boulevard carries a deep drainage ditch. Beyond barbed wire fences and the rusty winter tangle of bramble and hawthorn, the landscape on that side is open. Snowbound, it was a masked and costumed friend, both familiar and strange. *Oh, come on! I know it's you!* It woke up all the senses and sent them skittering on an urgent sortie.

The dark firs on my right no longer ran beside the road; they had been transfigured into a towering backdrop of snow-sculptures for the land on my left that swelled and rolled and billowed to their feet. Boulevards, ditches fences, all had been obliterated. The land had recovered its continuity, its contours melting one into the next, its borders erased. In the middle distance a white farmhouse grew out of the snow. Had its roof only been a little lower, the illusion would have been complete.

The road of course had vanished. I walked a medieval track, white and soundless, between waist-high snow banks tinged with blue, through a landscape that was at once perfectly still yet mysteriously in motion with, if you listened hard enough into the silence, a minuscule, a thousandfold crepitation. It breathed. The landscape and I were in a lock-down under the sky. On any other day the cloud layer would have been grey. Instead it was sickly white. It was as if the brilliant light from the snow, when it lay under bright sun, had been stored, now to evaporate and hang thin and diffuse in the sky, hueless. This watery pallor was not contained anywhere. It simply was, everywhere. It continued on down from the sky and hung above the landscape making the air itself wet — or was it the snow rising again in a cold vapour? The landscape was dissolving like a scene in a film. 'FADE to 1390'.

I had never felt more strongly the message that this is the same earth, the same sky, these the same elements that my ancestors knew. I could have been walking a lane in Cornwall, a track in Cork. The present world and its trappings fell away, cars, computers, movies, books, dentists, vitamins, cell phones, college courses, newspapers, pharmacies, vets, plumbing. Endangered species! The Olympics! The Ozone! Parliament Hill! The Middle East! Apart from the weather itself nothing could impinge on this day's experience.

A thin twist of smoke from the farmhouse chimney lost itself in the sky. It was not hard to imagine myself a peasant, legs wrapped in wool, a bundle of sticks on my back. I'd feel the same damp chill striking through, have the same thoughts of the glow of the fire, the smell of pine logs burning. I would not have turned a hair to have met a knave gathering winter fuel.

When I am writing a novel set in the past, I need to acquire some sense of the world into which my characters are about to step. Researching a novel set in sixteenth century Italy, I spent hours reading extracts of contemporary writings by scientists, artists, clerics and merchants as well as earlier works. I needed to know not so much what was on the point of discovery in their own century but what had been handed down to them, what was accepted then as given, familiar, what constituted received wisdom, common sense, the world as their mothers and grandmothers had known it. What kind of intellectual and spiritual property did they hold in common? They lived in a pre-industrial, pre-technological cosmos but they ate the same bread, picked the same flowers, stoked the same fires. What contentments rocked them to sleep? What kept them awake at night?

I returned again and again to the trecento, dipping into the letters of Francesco di Maro Datini and Margherita Datini liberally cited in Iris Origo's wonderful *The Merchant of Prato*. I took the Florentine apothecary Luca Landucci to bed, cosying down with the journal he kept between 1450 and 1542. This preparatory work of peering through time's telescope revealed more than I was looking for. I could see, distantly and imperfectly, some kind of stage on which my characters could move. I could discern, that is, a material landscape of sorts in its own intellectual and psychological climate. I was ready to send in appropriate emotional weather. But at times is was as if a hand reached out and turned my telescope the right way round. There they were in close up, these six-hundred-year-old Tuscans and oh look! It's us!

Family members bicker, whine and fret. Francesco and Margherita are so good at it in their letters that you wish you could see them in action on e-mail, exploiting its possibilities during their argument over whether Francesco cared more for his mule, dear God, than his wife. In the towns, the concerns and anxieties that animated or stalled the lives of our ancestors — who will be liable for the new tax, will the proposed causeway really improve the quality of life? — sound extraordinarily familiar. Pope Pious II sounds like your most curmudgeonly uncle. The students who so rankled him in Vienna in 1458 might have been in Halifax. They were more intent on food and drink than study, the pope complained, and roamed the streets day and night causing grief, their wits "completely addled by the shamelessness of women." We worry now about the car rather than the mule, the flyover rather than the causeway — but we worry.

Post-modernists have surely got it wrong. It's the surface, the visible, the concrete, that changes, the invisible, the intangible, that are immutable. The cast are signed on for the duration. Only the props change.

Change is a treacherous concept. Before you know it the adjunct "for the better" is tacked onto it. Because each generation believes itself to have gained greater mastery over its world than the preceding generation, there is a common assumption that we must be many times more comfortable, more attuned than our ancestors. We've come so much further, understand our world so much better. We've somehow sailed out of the fog of anxiety and fear that hemmed in our European ancestors. Yet it actually proves quite difficult to imagine exactly what fears a medieval peasant might entertain in her world that we don't. Hell clearly outranks all others but what about fears in this world? War? I can clearly remember at the height of the cold war looking to the horizon after seeing a flash (probably a transformer on the power line arcing or shorting out or whatever it is they do to enliven the time) and expecting, it seemed such a real possibility, to see the sky turn white with a light brighter than the sun. I can remember, too, a particularly vivid nightmare after Dr. Helen Caldicott, speaking in Victoria, explained the nature of death at ground zero and in each of the concentric zones surrounding it. In my dream I ran against an endless tide of streaming humans to reach my family caught at home — at ground zero naturally — when the explosion came. I ran all night it seemed until I woke, heart pounding with the alarm. The shadow of the night's desolate grief and dread persisted when I woke, and on each waking for many days after. It should, would still, were it not for denial which keeps us all insanely functioning. And famine? You and I with the luxury to consider the question may never experience it. But for almost a billion people today it's alive and at large, a savage reality for approximately one sixth (possibly the same proportion that obtained six hundred years ago) of the world, for whom it likely occupies nine tenths of their days. The middle ages cannot claim exclusive rights to hunger. Pestilence? Margherita kept a wary eye on the progress of the plague but resigned herself to its menace, which she likened to Judgement Day "of which we do not know whether it will come upon us by day or by night." But if Margherita lived now in any part of he world where AIDS is endemic, and both prevention and treatment are minimal, her fortitude might be sorely put to the test. And if she lived in Toronto? Better disease control and access to appropriate drugs is no protection against fear itself. Check out my vitamin cupboard. Better still, check out the profits of the pharmaceutical companies. Or simply watch what goes on in the market place as we scurry to buy sunscreen, insect repellent, hospital masks. Scared? With all that science at our fingertips, us?

Granted, there were vast unexplored, unexplained and sometimes too graphically explained reaches in the medieval world. It comprised both the visible and the invisible, the world of the soul, angels, devils, satanic powers, and a God who was not always in the best of humours.

Three-legged calves were potential links, as were falling cornices, freak accidents and strange fires in the sky. Urgent communication from the divine — if only you could figure out the code. Margherita's worst fear was the unknown and her worst enemy was her imagination. Mine too. We live surrounded by vast tracts of unknown. There may not be warlocks and werewolves out there but there are hidden, highly organized terrorist networks and mutant viruses as the media thrive by pointing out. Top of my own personal fear ratings are the biochemists. Not all of them, only those who indulge in impulsive, compulsive experimentation in pursuit of kudos or company profit. It's likely that I fear them as much as my, say, sixteenth century counterpart feared necromancers. I don't lie awake at night in a spasm of anxiety but whenever I hear of a team working flat out on some ill-conceived scheme, I'm filled with sinking dismay, leaden dread: what now? You just know it will turn out ill in the long run. I'd like, too, to posit that living with the bomb (to borrow a phrase from the sixties) has been much like living with an all powerful God who might on a whim and without so much as a whisper of warning visit mass destruction on us all, who might as it were go off.

Reading Landucci's diary one night, there was no suppressing the thought that he could have worked for the *National Post*. It was all there, from the floods to the fires to the atrocities perpetrated by foreign troops to the wild behaviour of youths who desecrate churches and show no fear of God, to the arrest of a man for the murder two years previously of a "young girl about twelve years old" whose body had been discovered by dogs outside the city gates. The violent, the strange, and the alarming always made the cut. And the weather never ceased to come up with something new. There were hot winds "as if it were July" in the middle of December causing all the interior walls of the houses to drip; tempests that destroyed roofs and uprooted trees, "twisting them like withies"; and, rivalling Montreal, a spectacular ice storm breaking branches of chestnut nearly two feet thick "so that those who chanced to be in the woods, thought the world was coming to an end, when they heard everything cracking, and the deafening noises overhead . . . and the stubble in the fields looked like organ pipes. The stacks appeared to be roofed with glass, and it was too dangerous for anyone to walk in the country. The farms were ruined for many years . . . It was incredible but true." I know how he felt.

My own education led me to believe that in the fifteenth century the bulk of the population would have shared a very meagre body of knowledge, much of which would have been drawn from some combination of religion, superstition, myth and erroneous science. Important work was being conducted in astronomy, botany, mechanical engineering, anatomy, mathematics, cartography, horticulture, agriculture, not to mention the arts of war and (in Europe) that age's own particularly hair-raising practice of medicine that had previously been in the hands of herbalists; but still it seemed fair to assume that most of it would have been unfamiliar to the unprivileged majority. In other words, in relation to the overall world view — that we from our long perspective can piece together through texts and artefacts and paintings — the average inhabitant of the ancient world knew precious little about it.

Our own knowledge, everyone agrees, has expanded with explosive speed and range — presenting us with a correspondingly enlarged universe. The net result, it seems to me, is that we're still a bunch of benighted peasants, knowing only a smidgen of what there is to be known about this existence of ours in a universe that now extends from the DNA in the cells on the soles of our feet to galaxies a billion light years away. We still walk with Margherita and Francesco on our own version of flat earth.

A Canadian takes a TV camera to the streets of America and for our amusement exposes the ignorance of Americans on Canadian politics and culture. But what if a Canadian were to take a TV camera to Burrard and Georgia at lunch time to ask a few basic questions about the human genome, DNA, genetic engineering, the properties of light, the transport of oxygen in the body, solar power, chlorophyll, or let's get simpler, the parts of a rose, the relation between the moon and the tides, the night sky . . . ? My own answers would make for fine entertainment. Our TV cameraman might be hard put to find a single Canadian able to correctly number, let alone name, the bones in his feet. And why would one want to? We know only what we need to know. Many of us rely on a separate race called experts to examine and describe our world; some of us don't feel a need to know. Creation does not need us to divine its secrets in order to perform its wonders. The show in all its complexity and beauty will continue with or without our understanding — or our tinkering.

Knowledge is a can of worms, or a more precise metaphor would be a clump, its form uncommonly like a brain except that on close inspection it is composed of a mass of tangled, intertwined wriggly tubes. The specialist can see a vast distance down the long and extremely narrow tunnel of her particular discipline and even peer around its blind bends. It's no more than a pipe, really, a pipelet, a mere tubule, but she has an inkling she can see all the way to the end. The specialist beside her for the most part doesn't hear her exclamations of awe and wonder but continues to look down his particular worm cast, equally excited by his own sense of being about to unlock its secret, travel its entire length. The rest of us content ourselves with getting a rough picture of the surface whole. We can see the various worms — fibre optics, genetics, nuclear physics, biochemistry — but they're all balled up and who knows where their ends are? What do you do on nights when you think about all those years, all those dollars (that could have fed people), all those lives staring down long wiggly tubules only to come up with nerve gas or a fat that the body can't metabolize or a soya bean that tastes like sausage or lipstick that stays on or a missile that can steer itself or a nuclear weapon that can fit in the palm of a hand or a pig that doesn't need to eat or a cow that doesn't need to shit (for whatever you think of will come to pass. We were sunk as soon as we reached for that apple) or chickens that need neither heads nor feet to lay? What do you do? You go out and you look at the stars and you break your heart for cold heaven.

❖

We live beneath the tailings of centuries of thought and enquiry, though we delude ourselves we stand on their slopes. We can scarcely breathe under the landslip of information. Sometimes, if I can crawl out for long enough, I indulge in a dream of innocence: to be able to walk abroad without our present science to explain and predict and without the intervention of the media, including print, to interpret and lie. And what *if* I should scuttle home and hide under the bed for superstitious fear of a two-headed toad?

That people of earlier times lived simpler lives is not in fact a view I hold, but I can see how the belief has arisen. It's such an attractive picture, to live each day with a supply of fat hours and a finite list of simple, self-explanatory, self-fulfilling tasks: rise from bed, fill chamber, wash, dress, empty chamber, feed mule, sup on bread steeped in broth, take mule and carry cheese and grapes and jug of wine to bottom field, plough field, sup on cheese, grapes . . . But only those on the lowest rungs of society had lives approaching anything that could be called simple — which for the most part translated as beggarly as well as brutish. The rest, in the period and the culture that supplied my reading, lived demanding lives within a complex network of relationships. Housewives, merchants, artisans, trades people all required a variety of specialized skills; the vital knowledge germane to each role was theirs both to acquire and impart.

Again it's this area of knowledge and information that gives rise to the illusion of living in a changed world. With the internet we are as close as makes no difference to a state of affairs where virtually the entire bank of human knowledge/learning is available to us — virtually. (That is, we can read it. Knowing does not necessarily follow from ingesting.) We career about on this fabulous new causeway with our mental windshields clouded by countless smatterings of information. But the highway actually takes us nowhere. We are on it forever. The more we think we know, the more we think we need to know.

In this, the acquisition of knowledge and the advance of technology are similar: each shrinks its own usefulness even as it expands its province. Both are a fool's game. The plank-thick pronouncement of a great dull Luddite? Probably. But some things you know with your heart. Here is one thing I know: that each one of us desires more time — and neither knowledge nor technology deliver it.

As an adjunct to writing, I walk every day, choosing an hour when there is little traffic, leaving my dog free to run alongside, my mind free to do its work without me. Since I have visited that late medieval, early renaissance landscape, I long more than ever to apprehend the world without these accretions of imperfectly absorbed knowledge. I'd like to set forth with a clear mind and no spattered windshield, no awareness of any world other than my own. I'd like to apprehend the weather, the hedgerow, the stream, the sun as the particulars of my world, props for my personal stage. I'd like to be Leonardo in direct hot-shoe contact with experience.

❖

I've just bought a little second-hand boat, a sailing dinghy, fourteen foot, gaff rigged. I love to say that: gaff rigged. I don't come from a nautical family and have never lived around boats. I'm starting from way back behind the line and will have to learn everything from scratch, the terms, the manoeuvres, the rules of the road. When I have learned a certain amount, my body of knowledge will look something like a home-made dock: bright new planks of acquired learning interspersed with gaping holes where intuition should be. It's not really intuition of course, that handiness you observe in those who have been brought up with boats. It's experience. It leaked into them in their youth. As children they were drip fed and didn't even know it. They thought they were playing; sometimes they thought they were helping. What they were actually doing, painlessly, was swallowing the complete package — hook, line and sinker.

My boat needs a few small repairs. I shall have to patch a split in the fibreglass and straighten out a kink in the aluminum mast. When I finally get her (her!) on the water it will not be for the purpose of fishing or racing or even to go anywhere. It will be for just being, the same experience as sleeping under the stars. It will be for the experience of oneness with my planet. Me and the wind and the water. And above all the air. I shall drink the air.

In the introductory lesson to the St. John's Ambulance Emergency First Aid program, you will be told at the outset, probably by the same two ladies in pastel blouses, navy skirts and sensible shoes who handed on this nugget to me, that there is only one way to die: suffocation.

❖

Everyday on my walks, particularly since walking that medieval track in the snow, one thing becomes clearer and clearer. The world does not change.

In May the hawthorn blossom still crests and foams over the hedgerows, wave upon wave of it breaking all along the roadside, filling the air with its scent of cats and sex and almonds. In June the dogrose still follows with its sweet correction (No, this. *This* is perfume.) fresh as a bitten petal. The cat still hunts at night. The calf still lows under the knife and the father sheds tears still at the sight of his new born son, already old, the lines of grief and laughter already etched on its crumpled face. The world does not change.

And how its constancy consoles. The world is in change but it does not change. The realization removes the grit (not the reality but its scratchy residue that scars vision) of global warming, toxic waste, the ills of mass consumption. It assures and reassures. It leaves the retina of the mind clear. The shadows of clouds still darken sunlit hills; bird calls still echo in the woods. Is this madness, this idiot ecstasy? This vision of constancy wilful blindness? The speed with which the world and we, (as products of the very environment we have created) are changing is commonly acknowledged. My recycling box is full of stories pertaining to it. It touches every conceivable discipline, every human endeavour, from learning to sport to business to art, to communication to agriculture. And no community is exempt. Even cultures only a step away from what the western world might consider medievalism find cell phones handy.

In October of 2002 I visited Shanghai. The drive from the vast gleaming airport was unremarkable: factories, flat land, wide highways, grey; each of us in the taxi waiting to be amazed by whatever combination of Qing Dynasty, Treaty Port and Communism our imaginations had already constructed. I was expecting to step out onto the Bund, the commercial waterfront where the great banking houses of

Europe set up shop in the 1920s in ponderous stone and brass-bound edifices which still stand, and whose public gardens once displayed the infamous by-law, "No dogs, no Chinese". Instead, we were taken just across the river to Pudong, where, to reach our hotel, the taxi ricocheted around the one-way system, turning and doubling back with all the logic of pin-ball. Amazed we were. We passed and repassed shining towers. We contorted ourselves to catch their height through the windows of the taxi, gasped to see their tops vanishing in foggy cloud. Pudong is jaw-dropping modern, a business centre built from scrubby marshland to glittering towers of glass and steel in just eight years. It is shiny and shocking in pink and gold and ethereal blue, a space-fantasy world of comic-book architecture where Spiderman and his friends might happily repair. No boring stretch rectangles upended here but towers stoppered like Art Deco bottles, towers sporting winged shoulders out of *Star Trek*, or pierced with holes, or crowned with gold. A slender silver ziggurat from Mars disappears into the high fog and the topmost sphere on the tallest telecommunications tower in the world — playful in pink and silver like a dream ride from the PNE — can only be guessed at. From marsh to space city — in eight years flat. How did we not know about it? All over our hotel, in the dining room, the breakfast bar, the lounge, even in the lobby, proposals and offers were in the air and deals were being struck by Americans, Canadians and Europeans whose companies were hoping to catch a ride on this economic tsunami. Sheepishly at dinner we lay our precon-ceptions on the table. Most of us admitted to wondering, when packing, if the hotel would have outlets for hair driers and razors.

One day during our visit we took a bus north-east of Shanghai on a highway that snaked and arced through a forest of plain concrete high-rise apartment buildings extending as far as the eye could see in all directions. After an hour and a half of driving, the buildings were still with us. The tops of some of them disappeared into the ever-present cloud, which we now recognized as pollution and which extended to the limit of vision. After two hours or so we arrived in what had been billed as a rural paradise. It wasn't, but I can tell you this: timbers still knew how to return birdsong to the ear, and rain still danced on the surface of stone. It didn't look as if the people had changed much either. Why would they? Why would we? For all the articles that tell us how our behaviours are adapting, our brains evolving to keep pace with the digital world they've created, parents still beam idiotically at infants. Infant laughter still makes heads turn, merchants still draw you by the sleeve. Quarrels still erupt, still draw blood.

But if I'm so certain why do I feel the need to insist so, to protest? Travelling to the People's Republic confirmed my belief in constancy but not before it had roughly shaken it. The press of people on the planet can be felt there. The hectares of high-rise apartments roll away from the bus window like fields of Saskatchewan wheat. Families stacked one on top of the other as far as the eye can see, and each one of them wanting to, working to, catch up with the west and go shopping. The world, that is, the great rolling planet and its diaphanous green and blue gown, both is and is not subject to change. That is the constant. It lives and breathes in a dance whose rhythms are aeons long. With each turn of the dance it sweeps creatures and plants within the folds of its gown, releases them transformed on the next breath. We tumbled out of those green and gold folds, naked and shining and we will be swept back in before we have turned a measure. The planet wears a living embroidery of movement and change, each life form intent on working its own thread, unaware of the whole cloth. The beauty of the natural world is that it lives in complete obedience to itself. Simone Weil said that absence of intention is the essence of beauty. The contention is easy to support. The firestorm is beautiful. So is the action of a moth's antennae. To look at a field of grass before it blonds away to hay, to see it in the late day bronzey pink in the low sun is to witness the perfection of obedience.

The constancy of the world fills me with gratitude — that I should be so lucky to see it, to know it, when I'm told, when I sometimes *feel*, it's on the point of flying apart. But of course that is the whole trouble. Our capacity (programmed or not is beside the point) to respond at an intensely personal level to beauty comes at a price. We could break here to argue here about what constitutes beauty, but I have no wish to. Certainly there are cultural and historical variants but put those aside and the question is truly quattrocento academic. Can we agree that a flamboyant sunset fills an empty space in us with a kind of desirous pleasure? For if we can't . . . then let us all crawl into individual caves and have done with it. The ability to respond both aesthetically and emotionally (though the sunset is deaf, mute and blind) is part of the steeply priced package of consciousness and self-awareness — or, looked at the other way, our self awareness, which has all sorts of hidden costs attached, comes with the 'free' and possibly useless gift of an ability to say Wow! Consciousness is a high price to pay for a hit of flaming sky, foaming sea. Self-consciousness is the highest price. Observing our own actions instead of mindlessly — or perfectly — obeying our biochemistry knocks us from a singular path. Instead we stand at the head of an endlessly branching trail, afflicted by choice. Yet isn't the flaming sky, the foaming sea exactly what it's all about? Sometimes, when a razzle of white breaks out along the ridge of a cresting blue-green wave, or a wind-swarm rushes the poplars and flips every leaf to silver against a liver-coloured sky, I think I would happily go barefoot all my days just to see it on demand.

The knowledge that we're personally implicated in the destruction of creation is a monstrous burden. It can be argued that being self-aware as opposed to blind bundles of biochemical impulses is our role and we are programmed to pursue it to its end. I've no quarrel with that. It's just depressing. We may be heading down a sequence of paths that lead only to a point of utter hopelessness. But I still feel hopeful, for exactly there, at the point at which we throw down our backpacks, throw up our hands and say "OK. You win," at that moment, when we all lie down and all roll over for dead, the planet will recover.

The planet is already impoverished by our presence. Our present numbers are enough to strain its resources, given the technological innovation that enables all of our destructive tampering and profligate consumption. And yet, and yet. We still have not found a way to unhitch ourselves from the web of life and *that* is the planet's faint hope clause: our place in it will be modified on a scale exactly proportionate with our damage to it. As we modify so we shall be modified. As we live so shall we die. Our industrial plants lace our water, our air with contaminants that kill us with cancer and liver disease; our rapacious agricultural practices bring us fast food to kill us fast. Jim Lovelock did an excellent job of identifying and articulating this self-correcting principle which he named Gaia. But you have to wonder why it took a scientist to figure it. Are we so blind?

Yes. We are blind as bats. It does take a scientist to conceive such thought. Scientists — using the term broadly to include all who stop, observe and attend, though they might not recognize a test tube if they saw one — are the best thinkers. They attend. Because they attend, they have the ability to see, as Ursula Franklin has put it "with different eyes". To say that scientists make the best thinkers is not in any way to revise my opinion that the practice of modern science is as bad for the planet as corporate greed, mass consumption or war. Modern science has fused with all three, entering an incestuous partnership where, by virtue of the funding that enables it, it enables them. The innovations of scientists are constantly winding each of these pursuits to new levels of destruction. We are in serious danger from scientists who though they have the ability to make the best thinkers don't actually think. They have goals instead.

We are blind and we are slow learners. The patient planet has been sending us the same message for a long time. The most observant saw it long ago without the aid of technology. The earliest recorded Western philosophers arrived at theories startlingly close to the principles confirmed by our own heavily-funded biochemists and molecular-biologists. Reason and intuition (which may be the simple product of attention) showed them that all parts of the created world are interconnected, sharing common elements and in constant interaction. They intuited the principles that govern the combination and the mechanics of elements, atoms, cells. Later, Plotinus might almost be describing the string theory of particle physics when he talks about soul: "A sympathy pervades this single universe, like a single living creature . . . Like parts lie not in contact but separated, with other parts in between, yet by their likeness they feel sympathy . . . "

But these philosophers truly were blessed with "different eyes". We may have to go far down the road to destruction, we may have to go, some still kicking and screaming to hang on to their toys, to the brink before everyone gets it. Perhaps we shall go over.

But there is this. When we have destroyed the small beauties of blossom and bee there will be others. Perhaps flames and raging winds. Perhaps glaciers roaring, careening through millennia, perhaps black waters fathoms deep in silent stars. Even if it is only the intricate arabesques of electrons or the precision mechanics of the cell's chemistry, all — everything that is left, that is starting anew — all will be possessed of perfect obedience. Just as the world even in its breakdown and decay performs word for word in accordance with the script — whose current translation is adapt or die — so the world we quit will continue to express its existence in Weil's perfect obedience, perfect beauty, only we shall not be there to see it.

I once tried soliciting a Christian fundamentalist for a signature on a nuclear disarmament petition. No, he said.

He couldn't sign. He was looking forward to the rapture. Similarly, but from his position as an atheist, my own son says the sooner we're gone the better. A student of biology, he stands in right regard of the complexity and beauty of the intricate workings of the life forms that surround us and considerable disgust at our disregard of their delicate mechanisms. But I can agree with neither. I was raised in a moralistic tradition and I cannot shake a sense of duty. For me, increasingly, duty seems to be allied to consciousness. Pierre Teilhard de Chardin believed that as we evolve we approach the fulfilment of our destiny: the consciousness of the planet. I like that idea. I like to think of a living, an aware, weave of human beings circling the planet with an undulating ever-changing, never-changing ever-conscious membrane. But if that is truly our purpose then we are sorely, mortally distracted. If humanity is the consciousness of creation then the planet is its body and we are driving it like a hard-drinking brawling party animal to destruction, at least in terms of a body that can serve us. The mother earth our children will know will be a body ravaged by excess, a body emaciated, impoverished, compromised and enfeebled by sickness, depleted, scarred, wrinkled and greying. As an organism it will like a corpse support life — but not its own consciousness.

Does it matter?

A nuclear holocaust of doomsday proportions has — no one quite understood why, least of all those who pressed the buttons — befallen the planet. Millions of years have unrolled. Jonathan Schell's republic of insects and grass has come to pass. A rippling sea of it has risen to wash the face of the earth. It is in constant movement under the winds that swoop and rush beneath the passing clouds. Micro-organisms seethe at its roots. Ancient insects lay their eggs, take flight and fall to earth. On some mornings the grasses are blown with a lemony light; some afternoons in winter their gold reddens and deepens almost purple. And bronzey pink. They shine again in spring. We are not there to see it. Does it matter?

What if our only function is to bear witness to beauty? Can you, could you bear the loneliness of the stars?

On a night in late September in the year of the big snowfall there was a lunar eclipse. I watched it from a little wooden deck built on low bank above the beach, my favourite place for moon-gazing. Strange and beautiful as it was, the eclipse seemed extraneous. The moon and water together are lovely enough, wonderful enough without magic tricks. I went to bed feeling inadequate that I had not been more moved. I woke to a morning of utter perfection. I had not seen its equal ever and went out early not just to greet it but to walk in it. The sky was awash in pink. I walked our long, straight road east towards the light. The dun grass fringing the fields was standing tall and crisp still in the damp. Up ahead, a barrier of mist hung across the road. Beyond it, the sky at the horizon glowed fierce and arduous between the dark trunks of the nearer trees. When I turned round, there was the lovely moon, returned to itself, full and whitely serene, floating in the pale pink-blue, a mistiness, an ethereal echo of earthly fog beneath it. On the walk back, the countryside was stirring. Geese chuckled intently, treading a turned field for worms. A blue jay was inspecting bits of bark by a trail's entrance. My son saw a

black cat leap along the ditch bottom like a dolphin. He
saw it.

❖

Animals and children are at home in the world. I
remember an afternoon spent concocting perfumes,
tearing rose petals from the blooms and pounding them
in jam jars with the handles of wooden spoons. The bruised
petals oxydized and the water turned to cloudy tea with
greyish bubbles at the surface. But I can smell now the
sweetness of the rose and my finger tips know precisely the
thickness and the silkiness of its petals the way the tongue
can never not know, once tried, the taste of violet.

On a holiday on the coast of Kent my sister and I
collected chalk from the foot of the vertical cliff face,
gouging it into tin buckets and mixing it to paste with the
sea water. We did this for no other reason than to experience this new substance, both hard and soft, to learn the
completeness of its white, unmatched even by the shells we
found at the water's edge.

And then there was a day in winter so cold that the water
in the ditches froze. This was England. We wore Wellington
boots with two pairs of socks. It was a fine day but the ditch
was shaded by a high hedge and stayed frozen. It was deep
and fringed with long straw coloured grasses that arched
across in places to make a tunnel. We climbed into the
ditch and ran and slid, ran and slid, further each time from
home. All day — perhaps — we skated the length of that
ditch and back, the length of that ditch and back. The
action of sliding reinforced the moment, the moment. It
reinforced the moment all day. If ever I have leisure to

make some kind of quality assessment of my days, that one will win a high rating. And one frosty Boxing Day I spent on horseback. And body surfing on a day of freakish wind at Cabbage Beach on Providence Island. And swimming in phosphorescence on a Vancouver Island summer's night. The formal celebrations that are supposed to mark the passage of years — the birthdays, personal achievements, weddings and anniversaries would rank well below. I've rarely been though any of these occasions with body, mind and soul connected the way they were when I defied the laws of physics and shot up the beach head first in a hiss of surf.

Adrenaline is a good conduit for cosmic voltage. It's the juice in the battery. For cowards like me it's easy to come by. Other people need to jump out of planes to get it. The motivation for the extreme sports enthusiast is all about achieving that connection, the point of total focus. The body likes that, says do it again. Or was it the mind? Total awareness equals total loss of self — equals total obedience. And perfect obedience equals beauty. And you are in it. You are it. The outside comes in. The boundaries dissolve.

In considering the world and my relationship to it I'm held spinning, like the child's toy I never could master, between two sticks, two issues. One is the desire to live a charged life, to walk with live wires trailing from the soles of my feet over the earth and feel the voltage of creation. The other is the suspicion that can never be confirmed that there is something more and with that the sense that I am far from home. The two go hand in hand; when one is achieved (momentarily), the itchy feeling of the other settles down. Here and now is suddenly enough.

"From a place I came That was never in time, From the beat of a heart That was never in pain ." More than one spiritual tradition can embrace the English poet Kathleen Raine's sense of longing for a forgotten Eden.

There is no comparing the space we normally inhabit and Raine's place where time expands, the mind focuses and life feels real. Hers is the place that mystics walk deserts to reach. There you escape the dank confines of the mind and thought's relentless formication over its mildewed walls. The walls crumble. You can get to it without chemical assistance by a number of different routes though sitting to meditation for two hours in a dimmed and silent room is hard. Sex can be too. So can being in a state of love or peril. And crawling across a vertical rock faces aided by bolts you've planted yourself. But walking is a breeze. So is watching the sky.

My dog gets there with no trouble. She basks. That 's' is no typo. She basks. On a sunny day I'll find her lying on her back, dead dog style, perhaps one forepaw turned down, her spine in contact with the earth. She's not sleeping. She's letting her body ride for free on the curved surface of the rolling planet and she's visiting the universe. And it's not just the sun's energy that brings this on. There are moments in a family, some odd five minutes in the kitchen when everyone touches down unexpectedly on the same landing pad, some sunny glade with a soft blue sky, a gentle buzz of insects, the drone of any other plane far, far distant. When it happens in my family, one of us will turn from the sink, the stove, and there the dog will be, collecting the cosmic rays, thrumming with the music of the spheres, basking in human harmony. I like to think this whole thing is circular, that when next I look in her eyes she'll release a little of that absorbed energy, add to my store for the day, make another soft landing possible.

There is a wall of glass at Vancouver airport where the earth-bound can see their dearly soon-to-be-departed after they have gone through the barrier. A blue cordon is supposed to keep viewers back but the glass is printed on both sides with recent kisses. I watched a family outside the departure lounge at our much smaller Victoria airport. The father was undisguisedly glum, the children were in tears. Inside the lounge their mother had pulled her chair close to, touching, the glass and endured the chaos of desire held in check.

We live our lives in that chaos of desire and it is so bad that mostly we repress it, or deny it, or deflect it. Some of us leap up and strangle our fellow passengers, the rest of us just go home and act out in the kitchen. Plate glass brings out the worst in us. And the best.

A Victoria poet tells the story of a toddler niece separated for weeks from her favourite companion, a Teletubby. When reunited, the child fell upon the toy, lay full length on top of it and began voraciously sucking its nose in a display of Blake's "gratified desire".

Apprehending beauty, don't we experience full consciousness? Don't we lose ourselves utterly and experience instead the thing itself? And when we do this don't we feel most fulfilled? I am not proposing a logical argument here; I can see the fallacy: when we are conscious of beauty we experience fulfilment therefore it is our purpose to be conscious of beauty. No. Purpose may be just

another human construct, like duty. Fine by me. I shall go
on seeking beauty.

❖

A few days ago, I woke from a dream of a conversation with
a Vancouver publisher. In the dream, he was bringing out
a book that "deals with the overriding question of our time:
'How To Think'" *What a good idea,* was my own thought on
waking. Timely. Thinking is surely harder today than at any
time in history. So much thought has preceded us. Worse,
it has been preserved for us in print. Worse still it has been
translated into our native tongues, made easily and cheaply
accessible. Impossible in our society to live a life
independent of the thoughts of others, to live according
to a schema of one's own devising, fashioned from direct
experience with the world itself. A body of learning existed
in ancient Greece, but the chances of escaping its reach,
of not being taught any of it, were surely higher for the
shepherd's daughter on Xanthos than they are now for the
sheep farmer's daughter on Salt Spring. Wouldn't you like
to walk just once in a field full of flowers and do some
serious wondering, attend to the evidence before your eyes
and come to your own conclusions? What ruins us for
wondering is that we know someone somewhere, some
specialist in a lab coat peering down a wiggly tube, has it
all figured. We will get even lazier now that the answers —
albeit *someone else's* answers — are just a mouse click away.

Besides, the very exercise is academic. We've told
ourselves that all answers can be dismissed as provisional,
as relative.

So much of our own thinking consists of virtual activities. The tape that is forever running in our heads is either scripting future events or replaying past. We remember conversations, rehearse phone calls, draw up timetables, agendas, proposals; we make plans, lists, plot victories, erase the record . . . None of these activities, and there are many more, take place in the here and now. We are so used to constructing our world that now that we have been made aware of what we do it is easy to believe that there is nothing that is not a construct. Easy too to fall in line with Buddhist philosophy and consider no thought at all as the most desirable and rewarding goal, the only reality.

Nothing is real.

Really?

I woke today from another dream . . . No, I'll start that again. I was happy to wake today from a dream of execution. Mine. In the dream my executioner was preparing me with a dry run for my own electrocution. I was co-operating with commendable aplomb — until I glimpsed a gate outside the window. What was I waiting for? As soon her back was turned I took off like the proverbial dirty shirt and was soon outside in the street, early evening sun of high summer enriching every house front, every tree, every fence post and my bare feet slapping out the theme from *Chariots of Fire* on the pavement. I drank the air.

As the dream unfolded I began to realize that my escape might be only temporary. The realization began to calcify into dread, then certainty. I met three children who had been gathering the bright yellow blooms growing among the shining stubble. They offered me some of the flowers and the thought came to me: *but perhaps this is all just a terrible dream.* Yet when I took the flowers I could feel their stems on my palm. I could feel the cut straw under my feet, and I knew with certainty it wasn't a dream. For the instant of waking, I could have wept for joy.

OF REMNANTS AND RICHES

STANDING IN THE MIDDLE OF THE MERCATO NUOVO, the tourist market in the centre of Florence, facing a vibrant razzle of silk that reaches from the grimy pavement to the stall's canvas awning, you can't help but hear a wistful echo from the city's magnificent trade in great bolts of luxurious wools and glorious satins and silks; for these silks — of every imaginable colour (an artist's palette!) — are all neck ties and head scarves, Gucci knock-offs, Versace look-alikes.

I'm in Florence for research. My head was crammed with it before I arrived. There is no shortage of information. At home on Vancouver Island, surrounded by heavy Douglas Firs and mists creeping in from the Pacific, or in an Internet café on Queen Street, you can inhabit the bright gold and lapis of fifteenth century Italy. Without leaving Canada you can discover every aspect of the Renaissance city, from the structure of its patrician society to the practice of stuffing food (almonds, figs, small birds, pies) inside other food (bigger pies, bigger birds, peacocks) to escape the sumptuary laws forbidding — well — sumptuousness.

I had enjoyed a virtual banquet of my own, from street plans circa 1490 to an artist's recipe for gesso, from slick reproductions of Botticelli to Cellini's first hand accounts of his scurrilous sexual exploits. I was suffering from overload.

Now, in front of this silk stall, I'm picking up another stream of information. Like a haywire short-wave radio, I'm picking up a scramble of German-French-English-American from the tourists all around, from the flyer advertising *Radio Maria FM88.6* and the peeling poster advertising *One Love Hi-pawa Concert Starfuckers Rock 'n' Roll*. The impressions pour in and mingle with the research and I feel like a flask in which a marvellous new solution is being mixed. It's a time-potion and present and past are collapsing.

There's no stopping it. Smell the spilled beer on the five-hundred-year old steps of the Ospedale degli Innocenti where the foundlings of the city were once laid at the tender (one hopes) mercy of the Guild of Silk Merchants. Catch the insistent beep of a hand-held computer game in the courtyard of the Brancacci Chapel. The words of the plaintive Englishwoman in the money exchange, *"I don't know what today is"*, suddenly take on a new significance. Everywhere I turn, the same alchemy is at work and the two streams are so mingled, so compounded that I can no longer say if what I see are sad tatters or splendid remnants.

For one of these shuddering time-jolts, come with me to the Palazzo Strozzi, fifteenth century family home of the fabulously rich Filippo Strozzi. 'Palace', with its connotations of gracious living is not the word for this rectangular pile of rough-cut stone built to brood over its wealth. It's a massive display of power and domination, a fortress. Its front door is thick enough to deflect a cruise missile. Its windows open from behind rigid iron bars. It's the Renaissance equivalent of the banking tower. But gleaming glass towers lack its square-shouldered solidity and are unlikely to be around in five-hundred years' time. The Strozzi Palace is the prize based not on electronic transactions but on muscle and sweat and gold coins.

Outside in the square, you can hear tinny music. There is no one about, but there, turning in the centre, in the long shadow of the palazzo, is a glittering, ornamented carousel, brightly lit. And if you stand a moment and allow the surprise to settle, if you listen for a moment to the music that no amount of tinselly sparkle can keep from sounding forlorn, you will begin to think positively medieval thoughts about the faux glitter of this world and the transience of wealth. And it will seem perfectly fitting that only May breezes ride the roundabout.

Nowhere is this violent collision of impressions, this speed-of-light rewind into "then" and fast-forward back again, more forcefully experienced than in the heart of the city itself. To come upon the Duomo, the glorious monumental confection that is the cathedral of Santa Maria del Fiore, suddenly — for there is no other way in this maze of narrow streets — is to be dazzled by the brilliance of its conjuring trick in a city of yellow stone. Nothing prepares you for the shock of the first glimpse, just as nothing, no visual image, prepares you for the blue of the Caribbean, or, back on the West Coast of Canada, your first killer whale, your first humming bird. Brunelleschi's massive brick cupola has been appearing over terracotta rooftops and disappearing behind yellow walls all the way, like the great shoulder of a shy, crouching giant. But, still, when you finally enter the square you can only be dazzled by its outrageous, improbable and improbably lovely cladding of shining white and pink and green marble. It is a conjuring trick in stone and you feel yourself at once as naive and as dumb struck as any fifteenth century traveller. A white-uniformed mounted policeman rides by and lets his coolly appraising gaze rest for a moment on the freshest and loveliest in the shambly crowd of tourists, and he is suddenly a proud *condottieri*, she a hapless maiden. But he rides on and we are out of 'pause' and fast-forwarding again to the present while she gets on with the serious business of sharing out gum to her friends.

The noise and the press of people here on the cathedral steps cannot be so very different from the atmosphere that would have prevailed on any one of the many holy days at this church built to accommodate thirty thousand faithful at a time. It is a human swarm. There is a certain olfactory swirl created by so many bodies standing in the sun: leather, vinyl, sweat, mint, shampoo (smells that may be less noxious but not less toxic), sunscreen, garlic, tobacco smoke, breath.

And everyone here in the Piazza wants to buy or to sell something at the great honey pot of the Duomo. The engravings and aquatints of later centuries have been replaced by colour prints and postcards of world-famous masterpieces. Challenged only by Rafael's much-abused cherubs, Michelangelo's *David* is top of the billboards. He is everywhere: whole Davids, parts of David, David's head, David's hand, and especially David's genitals, sometimes computer-enhanced and once wearing Groucho glasses and moustache. The buzz is all around the souvenir stalls just as it must have been around the vendors of relics and religious indulgences. Of course! It's so obvious. Tourists. Pilgrims. It just happens that in Italy our circuits are identical. No wonder we keep colliding. Look at us lining up at the doors to the cathedral museum, guidebooks like missals in hand, ready to be blessed by the experience of beholding genius. And there it is again, that collision: a newspaper headline announces that the Vatican has just issued an update on its inventory of indulgences, including one that might be earned from giving up smoking. Once you put on these lenses that look both ways in time, you can see forever. Sometimes they will deceive you. If you attend a mass here you will assume you are on the receiving end of a world class recording broadcast on a state of the art sound system — until you realise you are hearing the human voice, live, exulting against the arching stones exactly as it would have been heard five hundred years ago. Enough. It tires the brain and leaves it like an overloaded circuit board zapping and crazily sparking. We'll go, since he is everywhere beckoning, to see *David*.

The street that leads to the Galleria dell'Accademia is busy with pavement artists and poster sellers. Otherwise there is a pleasing lack of commerce. The Accademia exudes serious devotion to aesthetics. It is spacious and spare. The sense of anticipation in the foyer, before entering the *David* space, is palpable: this is high-tension art. We enter at one end of a long gallery, the colour of thin cream. At wide intervals down its length, two on each side, are the Prisoners, *I Schiavi*. These are four of the six slaves begun by Michelangelo for the tomb of Pope Julius II and never completed. Their silent presence is tremendous, almost in the original sense of the word: to excite trembling. I for one become instantly an unbeliever. Absurdly, in defiance of all documentation to the contrary, I can believe only one explanation for these human figures in super-human scale struggling eternally to free themselves from the stone: Michelangelo meant to leave them trapped. The symbolism of the work and its clear reference to the human condition is overwhelming, almost crushing. I find it suddenly necessary to sit down, to stay with them a while and listen to the reverberations of time trapped within the marble, the spirit within the flesh. Light pours into this quiet room from the long windows high on the opposite wall. And as I sit within my own experience inside this gallery, the windows, obeying some invisible electronic sensor, detect a threat to this climate-controlled environment and slide closed and the long white curtains glide silently together to shut out the late sun. The slaves imprisoned in stone, we in our technology.

We can pay homage to *David* in his semicircular space at the far end of the gallery, alone and splendid — but it is the slaves we shall take with us.

I need air. It's time to get out of the city with its maze of narrow streets. There is a bus that climbs the steep hill to Fiesole. It winds between the high stone walls of villas, brushing the thick foliage that overarches the road, and passing every so often an iron gate that teases with a glimpse of the view back towards the rooftops of the city. Standing room only in the bus. We all dip and bob inside, trying to catch one more preview of this new perspective of Florence. Almost at the summit, the bus stops in the main square of this small town. Fiesole is built on the site of an ancient Etruscan fortress and commands a truly wrap-around view of the valley of the Arno and the lovely undulating Tuscan landscape. Up here you can breathe, you can see. You can almost drink the limpid blue-green of the hills rolling away to the edge of sight. They entice you to walk out from the pretty square with its pollarded plane trees and its ancient town hall, its raised loggia hung with baskets of flowers, to separate yourself from the flock, become a wayward sheep instead for a while. It will be good to take one of the narrow streets that does not lead to a monastery or an amphitheatre, to breathe the air and imagine yourself into the landscape.

But already there is a distraction. A crowd is gathering over there by the ancient medieval cathedral of San Romolo. It's a wedding and the guests are arriving. The place to be is with the other tourists on a cobbled road that runs at a steep angle up from the tiny piazza in front of the cathedral and affords a perfect view of the Romanesque entrance. Everyone hopes for a glimpse of white, an ethereal airiness of veil, a drift of immaculate satin. But here first is the overture, a visual fanfare in the form of sleek limousines that slew to a standstill on the stones of the forecourt and release their elegant occupants, the wedding guests. And, oh, what guests! They know their part, are Oscar winners all, pausing to lay long pearl-tipped fingers on the crown of a shiny black straw, bending to adjust the blue ribbon on the seven-year-old's frock, checking the seam of the stocking (yes the seam, yes silk, in this age of Lycra) with a backward, over-the-shoulder glance that shows to perfection the arch of the eyebrow, the flutter of the eyelid. It's all a wonderful tableau — the wind whipping the edge of a narrow navy linen coat, the quadruple kisses of greeting, on each cheek and then each cheek again, the clipped trees in their great terracotta pots flanking the doorway, lemons glowing from their dark leaves. And here at last is our reward for our part as extras in this crowd scene — the bride untangling her dazzling self from the creamy leather interior of the car. Ahh! We make all the right noises as she emerges, and as she turns to bestow a smile on us there it is again, that collision in time. In five hundred years we have not changed at all but are as simple as any lumpen cloth worker or cloddy vagabond feeling pleased and possibly blessed by this smile from a bride.

Fl)rence has not changed and nor have we. The city itself has made that clear. The same sympathies and affections, the same appetites and the same vanities persist across cultures. The extravagant fashions in the Via Tornabuoni echo the opulent gowns of Ghirlandaio's women; the self-help books telling us how to live well are not so far removed from Savanarola's posthumous sixteenth century best seller, *The Art of Dying*; the clients at Eduardo Scissorhands, having bottles of colour emptied on their heads are not so different from the discontented Florentine ladies who treated their hair with a brew of orange peel, sulphur, and eggshells and went up to the rooftop terraces of their houses to bleach it in the sun.

The fresco paintings in the city down there affirm the parallels. Look at us and our long twentieth century love affair with film, and look again at all those frescoes. How they must have amazed and delighted with their new trick of perspective! Men and women so life-like "they lack only the power of speech" as Vasari put it, catching his breath in amazement. They were video; they fed the endless craving for story. Some, the great narrative cycles, are the forefathers of the comic book; some are loving biographies, others bald mythologizing; still others, cathartic and powerful, are richly composed cinematic shots in a magnificent drama that ends at the Last Judgement. Like film, they have the power to conjure the hellish vision from a box of colours — or to seduce with a dream of possibilities. Like film, they show the preoccupations, the obsessions, the fears and dreams of their age. And then there is sex and violence, the ecstatic Saint Sebastians bristling with arrows. He's still with us.

The bride has gone into the church. The bridegroom, looking as dashing and slightly alarmed as we knew he would, has followed. Across the main square, there is a narrow lane that leads out of the town and away from the crowd. An even narrower, walled, lane leads off to the right and curves around the face of the hill, opening on one side to a landscape of incomparable beauty and harmony. I stand at a stone wall above the garden of a house hidden behind a huge pine to my left. In front, the narrow garden falls away in a tumble of shiny spring grass tangled with wild flowers. There are two giant azaleas exuberant with blossom, a smothering of wisteria over an old wall, a small stand of foxgloves, some lilies springing from the bole of a peach tree. From this unkempt Eden wafts a perfume fresher than lilac, less spicy than wall-flower. A perfumer would die for the code of this scent. Beyond the garden, the land slopes away to a valley running across the line of sight, its far side rising again in a tapestry of greens and greys and white where the olive groves and vineyards and chestnut trees embroider this living fabric. All, all exactly as in any *Book of Hours*. Nothing changed. It is a harmony that caresses the eye and nourishes the spirit. The hill with its greens and silvers, its little blocks of ochre and its spears of darkest cypress rises up to a ridge where there is a village and a large villa and behind this another distant hill, and behind that another, on into the misty green-blue and palest blue-green. Nature making her own most eloquent plea for love — and allegiance.

Tomorrow I shall leave Florence. I shall walk to the station past stalls flaunting soccer scarves like the banners of ancient guilds. And from the train window I shall see an old couple of sixty years or so sitting on the stone bench in the station concourse. She will be lumpily shaped with poor hair and a weak chin like a character from an old TV show. He will be short and broad with a Roman face straight out of Asterix. Oh, but she will love him. She will have her head on his shoulder and he will have his arm round her, and now and then they will kiss. The past and the present will suddenly make sense. We haven't changed. We have the same burning loves as Petrarch, the same passions as Michelangelo — and we are still as much in need of tenderness as any della Robbia infant.

I take out my book. It's an intimate scene and I don't want to watch any longer. I'll give them back their privacy.

INSIDE THE DONUT SHOP:
A VIEW OF HISTORICAL FICTION

I DID NOT GO LOOKING FOR THE BOXER REBELLION as a subject for my first novel. Writing a short story set in the Caribbean (where I had lived for a couple of years), I needed to know more about local customs and religious beliefs so I had gone to my small local library to browse the shelves, something I love to do. It's as random as the internet for results. Because the database of the internet is so vast and that of most regional libraries so small, the search results in both have that same quality of quirk about them. Only two books away from voodoo practices in Haiti, on the same shelf, was the journal of a Canadian doctor in China. I picked it up idly and a memory stirred. My seven-year-old self stood beside me and we were transported back to my Roman Catholic primary school in England. "Faith of Our Fathers" was one of the hymns we sang at assembly. It took a good deal of ingenuity on the part of our teachers to explain what faith meant in the context of our modern, brightly-lit school and our reasonably comfortable lives, and a good deal of colourful storytelling to impress us with its importance. A particular teacher, in her zeal, thought to describe in detail the sufferings martyrs endured rather than deny their faith. She lavished attention on the story of the little Chinese boy, limbs hacked off one by one, who still refused, when asked, to deny that he was Catholic. I remember adding a special request to my nightly prayers after that — that, if the worst came to the worst, no one, please God, would ever ask me.

But back to the safety of the local library. This Canadian doctor was most emphatically not Bethune. I turned page after page barely able to believe the man's pompous, self-righteous, unquestioning and braggart tone. I think it was for his entertainment value that I took him home. I missed him when I had to return the book, but somewhere out of the brew of that moment and my childhood experiences, out of all those random influences common to writers, as well as out of some fairly purposeful research, he returned as a Canadian missionary for my first novel, *The Blackbird's Song*. I suddenly had the perfect material for an exploration of something that had long interested me, the relationship between faith and delusion. As well, I had a dramatic context for a good long look at a particular branch of western imperialism in action.

I arrive at any book by the same rambling, tangled route: mind-wide-open reading, dream and memory, watching and listening and sometimes stubborn refusal of the subject even when it starts to call. The way includes rest stops during which an accretion of images and ideas begins to form around the subject. And then we're off again and here come pure chance, helpless surrender, failed attempts, coincidence, and sudden swerving off the road to scribble down an idea before it vanishes. All of it builds a monumental hunger. With luck I happen on the donut shop at exactly the right moment.

Members of my husband's family love to tell how his French great-grandmother rowed with her children across the English Channel to escape the Franco-Prussian war. It's a great novel, ready-made, and I set out to write it. On the way, reading Alistair Horne's book, *The Fall of Paris*, I came across a reference to an advertisement in the *Times* for a Paris apartment "For the benefit of English Gentlemen wishing to view The Siege." (Already, in 1870, war as spectacle, war the reality show!) There, again ready made, was a character I wanted for my own, the kind of languid, callous fellow — keen on his creature comforts but as careless of his own safety as he was thoughtless of others' — who would answer that ad. Meanwhile I dreamed the beginning: "All the fishing boats at night out to the wreck — each with lights." Four nights later another dream: "A young man, blond, a soldier, pale, dragged behind a cart, hurting. When at last they cut the ropes, he was glad to die. Relieved." And then there were the photographs, for me always the best source of inspiration during research. The British photographer Julia Margaret Cameron (though she worked a little later) caught my attention. She was possessed of practicality and application but produced portraits informed with an unearthly Pre-Raphaelite air. Someone else demanding a role. But you can't accommodate everyone. You take what you need — that photograph of the child with a pair of swan's wings stuck on its back! — and toss the rest. Louise Michel, the fiery "Red Virgin" of the Communards, tried to elbow her way in too. She makes only a cameo appearance as herself but is wholly responsible for Madame's adolescent daughter burning with revolutionary zeal. Now I had something, suspiciously like a love triangle, that could try the notions of loyalty and duty and I fed it with everything that came my way. No room in the boat now for the Holdstock grandmother and her kids. Into the English Channel with them. In fact no room for the boat at all, though I shan't be surprised if the story surfaces again some day.

You could say the conception of a novel is something like an inebriated sexual encounter at a long and noisy party. Afterwards, it's clear something transpired but even when you're holding the baby in your arms, you'd be hard put to pin down the moment. Writers are such promiscuous readers, such voracious auditors. They're the local nympho-maniac lying down for every story that comes her way, the local rake taking whatever he needs, ruthless when he has what he wants.

"Why on earth?" — with the implication, "What could have possibly possessed you?" — is a question I've been asked more than once about my choice of material. Sometimes it's accompanied by the more kindly, "Is that something you've always been interested in, then?" I'm touched by the faith that there must be an explanation for this mildly dysfunctional behaviour of mine, this holing up for five or six years with the dead. No one I've ever loved, lived or broken bread with has ever had even a fleeting glimmer of interest in Boxer Rebels or Paris Communards. What they find hard to believe is that neither had I — before I began the books. And their questions were the ones I'd asked myself over successive novels, until I stopped long enough to observe what I was doing.

Every option of treatment and technique, every option of theme open to the writer of contemporary fiction is open to the writer of the historical novel — something that is often overlooked when historical fiction is considered as a self-contained form. In point of fact, there is so much of it about, and in such variety, that it hardly merits separate examination. Even if we unhitch the trailerful of costume dramas that causes people to say, "I just love — " or "I can't stand — " historical fiction," the parade is long and lively, a motley troupe confounding a host of works not normally considered historical — Michael Ondaatje's *In the Skin of a Lion* and *The English Patient*, Beryl Bainbridge's *The Birthday Boys*, Pat Barker's *The Ghost Road*, Katherine Govier's *Angel Walk*. It includes novels that are overtly historical but rarely categorized as such — Thomas Mann's *The Holy Sinner*, William Faulkner's *The Unvanquished*, William Golding's *The Inheritors*, as well as others sometimes mistakenly considered contemporary with the author — *Les Misérables, War and Peace* — whose world actually pre-dates the writer's birth. It also includes the work of those Hermione Lee calls "the historical fabulists of the post-colonial world" and, she might have added, of the post-patriarchal world. Here writers like Angela Carter and Rikki Ducornet stand alongside Peter Carey, Douglas Glover, Timothy Mo, Caryl Philips. And on and on.

None of these exists to provide what some publishers suggest readers are looking for, that is, "a window on a former world". It's always a mistake to turn to novels for that, informed as they are with the writer's every neurosis and obsession. Far better to turn to contemporary journals or letters, or at least to the historian who has combed them through and can interpret them with skill, someone of the stature of Alistair Horne, Christopher Hibbert, Iris Origo, Eugene Weber. These are the writers whose scholarship and integrity allow them to offer a picture as close to a presumed "authentic" as we could hope for. The historical novelist — like any other — is better equipped to provide a window on the human heart, by which I mean that strange receptacle for hopes and loves and dreams and detestations, fears and ambitions and a view perhaps as to how it might be carried about the world, among others possessed of the same volatile package, and yet survive. Whether it's done in a contemporary or a historical setting is almost irrelevant.

Ultimately 'historical fiction' is as sweeping and useless as any label stuck on literature. *I, Claudius* is so much more than a historical novel — just as *Oryx and Crake* is more than speculative fiction; *Lives of Girls and Women* is more than women's fiction and *No Great Mischief* is more than a Canadian novel.

A novel's foundation blocks are time and space — that is, place. Its authenticity is achieved through the many small details that are set upon them. Jane Urquhart, addressing an audience at a public reading in Sidney before she read from *Away*, heaved a great sigh and proceeded to tell us how difficult the work was. I knew what she was talking about. With each new novel, daily further from the point of embarkation, you begin to rue the day you ever set out. A whole world, of which you know nothing, has to be created out of thin air. You are forced back again and again onto the research of scholars. Your character wants some light to read a letter. Did he light a candle? What with? When was the first match? Where would that flint thing-y be kept? Or did he have a lamp? Oil? How did he get to it in the dark? And where did he pull that letter from anyway? Were pockets invented? It's all very tedious and you wish to just get on with your tale. Even when it's simple, it's not.

Changing language and contemporary notions are a constant hazard. "Pencil" and "towel" are both ancient words but use them in a Renaissance setting and you're in danger of yanking the reader back to the twenty-first century with yellow school supplies and co-ordinated bathrobes. It can take forever sometimes just to get a character out of the house in the morning. It's not surprising that you find yourself one day reading until three in the morning on the subject of, say, nineteenth century salvage practices, with specific reference to getting ships off rocks by means of something called warping. You don't want to be. You would much rather be reading a good novel — preferably contemporary — or sleeping.

But these concrete details are straightforward obstacles. It's relatively easy to find out how it was done and then write it. The difficulty pales in comparison with resolving the central problem: trying to recreate a vanished sensibility that in any case is, first and foremost, only a construction of our twenty-first century minds. Henry James said practically all there is to be said on the subject in a letter to his friend Sarah Orne Jewitt, warning her (as he would) against attempting the thing. All 'historic' novels were necessarily doomed, he believed, to what he called a "fatal cheapness" since an authentic representation of a former consciousness is an impossibility. It is not possible, he warned, to recreate a sensibility in which half the furniture of the modern consciousness is missing. He's right, of course, and states his case convincingly, ending with the dispiriting observation that even if you try, "it's all humbug." But even more to the point, I would say, is the difficulty of recreating that former sensibility with a mind in which half of the original furniture is missing — the newness of Darwin, say, or the feel of a blue paper cone of sugar. Alberto Manguel has written in detail of the 'language' of medieval and Renaissance paintings, a language we've now lost. How did it feel then to stand in front of a religious painting and be able to read it? How did it feel to be unable to read, to write? My children find it hard to imagine waking in a house whose windows have been frosted overnight — on the inside — with ice.

So there, before you even start, is the most fundamental challenge: how to step into that other consciousness, see with those other eyes. And yet. Isn't all novel writing a stepping into the consciousness of others? What James was saying in effect was that though some attempt may be made to reproduce the concrete world, the inner world (Forster's "life in time") may never be known. But hold on a minute. Didn't he attempt to reproduce the inner world of the young women who people his novels? He was apparently undaunted by the fact that their experience of the external world must have been vastly different from his own. All individuals are the product of the particular set of circumstances they inhabit. Is it really any cheaper to step into an earlier consciousness than it is to step into one prescribed by another sex, another place on earth or in society? What if I try to enter the consciousness of a homeless youth sleeping in a doorway on Yates Street? A cheap trick? Or a necessary one?

These questions carry echoes of the contentious issue of voice appropriation that in its misconstrued form haunted and hobbled Canadian literature in the 1980s. They're not unrelated. But none of the questions will stop writers stepping in and out of place and time and body. Wasn't there a novel in the 1990s written from the point of view of a blue bowl? If you could write a novel in the voice of an autistic child and come even close to conveying a sense of his world, would you be deterred by the question of appropriation? In life, outside the novel, our truest moments, mine anyway, are those when we know without a doubt the joy or the elation or the fear or the sadness of another. Imagination is my direct route to you, yours to me.

So, yes, there's justification for attempting the leap, but the original question remains. Why incur the additional difficulties posed by a displacement in time, or place for that matter? Clearly it's easier to write the world when it's at your fingertips. Why leave your home territory at all?

Penelope Fitzgerald is not widely known in Canada. She began writing late in life and quickly earned recognition with her extraordinarily light and cool prose, winning the Booker Prize for *Offshore* and going on to establish her place among the very best British writers. Her novels go after the big questions. They're slim silver-tipped arrows aimed at metaphysical thunderclouds.

Two of her books are set in previous centuries. They're rarely, if ever, referenced as historical, though they set a standard for the form that is beyond most writers' reach. Her worlds seem to exist beyond the text. The details are sharp but never superfluous or intrusive; they manage to appear integral to — well — everything. This is no easy feat. Two obvious questions follow, how? and why? No one has yet been able to give a satisfactory answer to the first; Fitzgerald's elusive skill is the literary equivalent of sleight of hand. I suspect that her personal qualities — detach-ment, irony and hope — are the perfect match for this form. As to the second question — why? — she herself

170

neatly forestalls it with the epigram from Novalis that opens her novel, *The Blue Flower*. "Novels arise out of the shortcomings of history."

Novels are able to question what history presents as fact. And novels can offer answers to the questions history leaves us. All the lost voices. There is a certain kind of writing that arises from a desire to restore voice where it was denied. I know when in my own work I was stricken with a spate of short stories grounded in the Old Testament, I was motivated by a sense of injustice on behalf of all the marginal characters, especially women, whose stories were never told. The shortcomings of the Bible.

But in art there is never only one reason for choosing a particular path. Michael Billington, theatre critic for the Guardian, wrote that the test of a history play was "whether it both pins down the past and reverberates in the present." His 'test' also describes another rationale for the form, "making the past a metaphor for the present." Sometimes, or perhaps just for some writers, the present won't do. It's too close to us. I hold my hand up in front of my face and touch my palm to my nose. I try describe what I see. Present issues get in the way of vision all the time. All I see is that big obtrusive thumb. Historical fiction deals with the problem. It's a lens not so much for viewing the past but for viewing the present. It removes ideas from the trap of immediate social issues, leaving a path open to the questions that might lie at the root of those issues (and will likely persist even when our attention is diverted to the next current concern).

Like any other literary form, historical fiction, may be either extrovert or introvert in character, examining either the individual within society or the individual as a mortal — and mortally aware — being within the created world. The fiction that looks outward is sometimes washed with a vaguely didactic intent. If it deals with the recent past, and especially if it concerns social conditions, it may be an attempt to examine cause and effect, or a way to illuminate a route to positive change. It's often revisionist, adjusting the received version of the past and reinterpreting events or amplifying them in the light of contemporary positions. Barry Unwin's *Sacred Hunger* won the Booker Prize in 1992 for just such a work. But conventional social realism set in the past can all too easily be haunted by shades of earnest 'young adult' fiction. It often works best when it's pushed over into fable, a strategy that's also well-suited to the philosophical novel.

Fiction that looks inward, the novel of the human heart (the psyche, the emotions) may be said to transcend time in the sense that its concerns will be the same as those written about five hundred years ago and those that will be written about five hundred years hence. But in each case the writing will arrive at the reader only through the filter of contemporary consciousness, regardless of when the action of the novel takes place.

This is the kind of writing that interests me, believing as I do that there are indeed constants to be reckoned with in human history and that literature is the place to do it.

It's this dimension of the novel that Stephen Henighan has overlooked in his collection of thoughtful and provocative essays, *When Words Deny The World.* For Henighan, the novel functions, must function, as the voice of the writer's own time and place. Historical fiction, on those terms, is excluded from serious literature and Henighan is stubbornly blind to the form's potential for anything other than "didactic nostalgia" or spectacle. Consumed with a thoroughly Canadian anxiety over identity, Henighan regards historical engagement — really an engagement with society and the politics of place — as a fundamental undertaking, a duty, almost, of the novel. By contrast there are writers in countries with more urgent cause to examine national identity who nonetheless hold a view diametrically opposed and who believe literature should transcend exactly those questions. Gao Xingjian, the Chinese writer awarded the Nobel prize for literature in 2000, is a powerful champion of this view. He advocates a literature beyond politics and ideologies, one that serves only "the voice of the individual", whose primary source is "feelings". Deeply suspicious of the attempt to stress national character or cultural features, he insists that literature must cross national boundaries.

In his dislike of historical fiction, and his demand for a literature that defines us now, in a political context, Stephen Henighan, it seems to me, overlooks completely the novel of ideas. For me, historical fiction is a means of entry to an idea to be explored. As well, it also happens to be a creditable route to self-forgetfulness, the one indispensible ingredient for art of any kind, the one trick the writer must learn in order to speak directly to the reader.

❖

While writing my (historical) novel *Beyond Measure*, I kept a journal of notes detailing some of the mental processes. Nowhere in my journal did I read any entries about the difficulty of pinning down the past. Henry James was so right when he identified it as an impossible labour — and so wrong when he defined the historical novel by that labour. His whole letter to Jewitt seems curiously off target. Writers of serious fiction who happen to locate their novels in the past are not trying to recreate the past (they have other things on their minds); that's just a chore that has to be completed, with varying degrees of thoroughness and success, for the real work to get done. Nor are good writers of contemporary fiction bent on defining, describing their times; they just happen to accomplish that while they wrestle with their individual angel — or demon.

And there will always be writers, even novelists, who do in fact feel as if they are just "passing through en route to eternity or oblivion" (terms I'm not using in connection with their careers . . .) They carry with them a consciousness of the long perspective. They — all right "we" — believe in good faith that our ills and issues, our quarrels and our endlessly repetitive tragedies, all the matter of our daily lives and our daily "news" are merely contemporary manifestations of our deep disorder, "the trouble" with us. For us, using the medium of fiction means being able to contemplate our predicament without going mad. Greed is the issue, ambition is the issue, meanness and mendacity and a propensity to inflict harm are the issue. And all of it is the poisonous product of a terrible commingling within us, consciousness of mortality cruelly bonded to a consciousness of beauty. Transient political systems and social structures, viewed in long perspective are as much current fashion as doublet and hose or platform shoes. The novelist who disengages from contemporary history might do so in order to try on something more than the political or the social wardrobe of the day. It's not globalism or corporatism or capitalism or communism, not neo-conservatism or liberalism or feminism — it's what drives us to ism-ize in the first place. And it's whether ideology per se merits a chunk of our time on earth. It's moral philosophy.

ON WRITING HISTORICAL FICTION

Aug '97
She must have some place in a procession/feast
She is used as an artist's model
She identifies with St. F. of A[s]sissi

Those were journal entries I made while considering the character of the mottled girl, Chiara for my novel. I already had the milieu. I already had, or thought I had, two of the other characters. But the casting about for a bite is evident. For me, historical fiction is never a representation of the lives of historical figures. My own obsessively scrupulous make-up forbids it. I would be crushed by the responsibility of representing a historical figure both fairly and truthfully, fearful of distorting the past. Like my friend, the late Rona Murray (we had several conversations on the subject), I'm a fiction writer who can't lie. Having someone misrepresent my own intentions or motives is for me about as bearable as having my teeth drilled. For that reason I have to create my figures anew, even if I do steal from the lives of their progenitors. Thankfully, I don't use all the ideas that suggest themselves in the working journal.

September 5

She is probably a slave although this will create problems,
being a giant step towards melodrama. I shall think about
it. For a considerable time now this novel has been developing.
I had set out two (?) years ago to write something about BC
Brideships. One of the passengers/brides-to-be with a flawed
skin but it simply would not take root and I had to go where
it was calling me. Italy! Artemisia Gentileschi. 16th C. The
disfigured woman to be her servant. And then the Vancouver
Art Gallery exhibition on the human body. Vesalius.
Anatomy. And, strangest of all, Julie Birchill's hilarious and
horrific article in Punch, *"Babies With Test Tubes."* (In this
article, Birchill tears the respectable face off certain
kinds of scientific research that subjects animals to
unimagined levels of brutality, the "Babies" in this
case being the scientists themselves, the test-tubes
their dubious toys.) *The passion that had been missing*
in my first idea returned. I know this work has to be about
cruelty. Cruelty and Beauty. Beauty and Cruelty. Not, I
hope, the cliché of the agony and the ecstasy but something
more complex. Our basic flaw, our inner flaw (the outer
[being] our disfigurement) that persists in destroying the
good and the beautiful in its insistence on exploitation for
personal gain, whether wealth, soc. stature, artistic develop,
science or, simply, kudos.

And so the work became not how to represent Artemisia,
but how to make bits of Artemisia's story serve these ideas.
The words 'cruelty and beauty', sometimes 'terror and
beauty' became the pendulum that swung without ceasing
through the writing of the book. Or the tolling of a bell.
In the heat of it all I thought it terribly original. The

following year I would go to Italy to get the feel again of Firenze. I left the family for that trip and went alone, purposeful. One afternoon I stopped in the Piazza Santa Croce to take an espresso at one of the outdoor tables of a huge cafè. Behind me, to my left, a man and a woman were talking poetry. Their conversation, in English, or rather, American, jumped out from the music of the Italian all around. I could not help but hear that they were poets. Laurence Ferlinghetti and Anne Waldeman had been in town, I knew, for a reading the day before I arrived. I'd have liked to turn round and talk with them but the intrusion, the crashing boredom (for them) of meeting yet another writer in a world full of them . . . And then someone reached from behind my left shoulder towards the book on my table — Luca Landucci's *A Florentine Diary* — and a man's voice said, "That's a book in English, you're reading?" The three of us talked for a little while. Yes, I was there for research. Yes, a novel. What was it about? "Ah," said Mr. Ferlinghetti, "cruelty and beauty?" And then, as if pondering, "Hmm. Beauty and cruelty." There was an extremely long pause. To this day I haven't figured out whether he liked the idea and was thinking of dashing off another poem or whether his response meant: "Hmm. *Those* old nags."

'98

Feb 13th

The strange way of this book's writing. It takes me two, almost three hours sometimes to spiral in on the act and then what I write is some central power point of the narrative, immensely (to me) powerful so that I have to sometimes get up mid-sentence, mid-word, walk across the room and come

back snatch up the pencil and continue, the words coming
fast, in a rush . . .

What has happened of course at that moment is that the
indispensable state of self-forgetfulness has arrived. Often
it comes when I'm looking away, intent on some logistical
problem, some nuisance of concrete detail that I have to
nail in place before my characters can go about their
business. In other words it's the form itself that creates the
conditions conducive to creating. In this, strange as it may
seem, historical fiction performs for me the same function
as poetry or indeed any other artistic imposition, any other
set of arbitrary constraints I might, like the members of the
Oulipo, dream up. It gets rid of the tyrannical self, the
pushy, insistent ego. The very difficulty and challenge of
the task frees up the mind and creates space. It allows the
imagination to take flight. Harry Matthews in an essay
published in *Brick* in 1997 has put it another way. Working
under severe restrictions, he says, "guarantees that the
unforeseen will keep happening. It keeps us out of
control." It distracts us in other words, from ourselves.
Before we know it, he says, we find ourselves writing the
hitherto unimaginable — "things that often turn out to be
exactly what we need to reach our goal."

Dec 2
Two extraordinary — what? signs? A couple of days ago,
reading Cellini I find his reference to the youth Asciano,
"so lovely" that all who behold him are moved "to love him
beyond measure."

Then, a few days previously, my visit to the fresco artist,
Marie Allison and her advice to my son, who was working

*in fresco, to soothe any burning from the lime with yoghurt.
This a really extraordinary sign for me since I have already
written [Orazio] lying in agony [from the lime] on a divan
with arms extended to either side and hands soaking in oil.*

About as extraordinary or interesting, I should imagine,
as someone else's dream next morning, but the point is
that the preface for my book, that was not to appear in the
Canadian edition, stated that I wanted the book to be not
a novel, not even a historical novel, but a flight of the imagination, and the spur for all that breathlessness in the
journal entry was the fact that these recurring coincidences
acted as validation for trusting the imagination.

A few days later I would come across more confirmation
when a monograph I had ordered through the library
service arrived. Iris Origo, describing Tuscany slaves in *The
Domestic Enemy*, writes that many were marked "by scars or
tattooed patterns on their faces" and she quotes a bill of
sale that describes a female slave with "many moles in her
face." I underlined the words. I'd already "invented" my
mottled slave. I'd have to wait a few more years before I'd
come across the ultimate validation of the creative process,
a reference to one Mary Sabina, a slave both black and
white, recorded in the eighteenth century by the naturalist,
Buffon.

It is not possible to imagine anything. Everything you
can imagine already exists, or will.

Feb 16
*I think there is some more (more) terrible material that I am
going to include. It concerns a horrific incident (actually
from the war in Bosnia-Herzegovina). It is so terrible that*

*I am reluctant to face it, also hesitant because I feel humbled
by it. It demands writing of power and stature that will be
able to find the intact humanity beneath the mess of gore[,]
that will in some way be able to restore some measure(!) of
beauty to the human face in its extremity.*

As it happened I included two twentieth century incidents,
both instances of extreme cruelty. I don't think I could have
dealt with either in a contemporary context without
succumbing to the temptation to climb into the pulpit.

July 3rd
*Since the last entry, I have been to Italy and back. The
journey has given me the confidence to take the leap (in time
and place, in my imagination) but it has not given me new
material. My material comes, as always, from my reading:*
      *— gold was considered as a 'good' thing, good for
anything. It was taken internally to ward off plague.
Golden pestles were used in preparing medicines.*
      *— the use of sulphur, eggshells and orange peel to
bleach hair.*

Everything is absorbed. I didn't use either of those snippets.
They went, though, to join the rest of the trivia that helps
to build a sensibility, the first a touching example of both
hope and faith as well as yet more evidence of man's
chronic presumption; the second a good indication of the
importance of appearance, a sample of what might really
have been on the minds of the laity when they weren't
worrying about judgment day.

Mar 9th

A new thought. It may be the answer to a problem that has been plaguing (ha) me since I began: how to avoid the childishness implicit in the artifice of the historical novel? How to deflect or forestall the 'pull-the-other-one' response of the modern reader? It may be that I have to openly address the reader. There may be a sort of veil or web within which the story is caught.

The journal is full of this kind of worrying of the form, evidence of how the mind becomes wholly preoccupied with wrestling with the constraints. The next entry clearly shows that Oulipo effect at work:

Mar 11th

Chiara. It is her story. People are revealed to her as organs are revealed to PP. Each character has another side to reveal. Nothing (no one) is as it seems.

The entry goes on with more revelations (to me) about my characters and even begins to throw light on the ending. Searching for the 'veil' actually gave me my main character and a whole lot more.

Apr 6th '99

At Queenswood House . . . A positive yearning to be here since I discovered the solid base of my book — it's a tale! — and so see my way forward. I shall tell my tale and tie up all the loose ends . . .

Apr 18th
. . . The form is becoming clearer. It will be the language
of the Fairy Tale certainly and it will be devoid of all psychol-
ogizing. For who can know? I want only to reveal the beauty
in the terror.

Though I did not in the end use language peculiar to the fairy tale, I did use its very particular voice. In a tale nothing is relative, nothing positional. It is as it is. Things are as they are. I cannot think of approaching any dangerous metaphysical question without this armour. Elsewhere, I have used fairy tale in its "pure" form for just this purpose — just as other writers, who don't work in the genre, have made use of detective fiction or the ghost story. Harry Matthews thoroughly understands the mechanism at work here. Again in his *Brick* essay, he recognizes that before the Oulipo and their elaborate self-imposed conventions, other writers were already setting themselves constraints by choosing particular forms — pornography, the fairy tale, parable. He could most certainly have added historical and speculative fiction.

May 7th
How all my days now are filled with this book. I know that
it is not beauty and terror but beauty in the terror. Beauty
revealed.

A long passage follows in which, on an evening charged with Hopkins' grandeur and glory, I had encountered someone with a physical defect of the most severe kind.

And this fellow? His affliction To endure it is to be part of the complex beauty of the world. To strive with it and still endure is to reveal the beauty of the soul.

Clearly I had been reading too much Weil, as I'm sure the "fellow" himself would have been more than ready to tell me. But the entry does show how life lived pours into a work, even if it is set in another time, another place. And the work pours into life. As in all novels, the real matter is not, is never the lives of the characters.

Dec 6th

Have begun laying out (!) the novel on the breakfast room table. It is very difficult work and I think I shall never again approach a book in the same cavalier fashion as I did this one — gaily typing "new" each day and beginning a wholly new disconnected passage, flying only on faith that one day the glue, or the mortar would be there to stick it all together. Very difficult work. I should have stopped a third of the way through to make these initial decisions that are the very basis of everything that follows.

Each morning I would pore over the chunks of text, shuffling and rearranging. That Christmas one of my sons gave me a one thousand piece jigsaw puzzle of *God Creating Adam* from Michelangelo's Sistine ceiling.

2000

May 8th

The novel is now laid out on the bedroom floor in a long white 'J'. The most difficult work this piecing together but

*perhaps that hook at the bottom of the 'J' is significant. I
have turned a corner. I think it can be done.*

This is the same year we have Alistair McLeod to read at
the Sidney Reading Series. I experience a sharp pang of
envy when he tells me he would never begin a piece of
fiction without knowing where he was going. He says he
likes to just take the wheel and keep going, "sort of like
driving to Kamloops, you know?"

*Jun 19th
The significance of the 'foetus' can be related to the terror
and the beauty of birth itself.*

This bit of illumination seems to have come extremely late
in the day. It becomes a kind of fulcrum for the novel though
at the outset it was non-existent. I really feel that if I'd been
driving to Kamloops at the time, I might have missed it.

*2001
July 18th
Yesterday I fanned the novel out on the floor.*

Again? Still?

*July 24th
The novel is finished. I delivered it personally to Hilary in
mid-August. Very difficult to hand it over. Not sure I could
entrust my baby . . .*

And I said, afterwards, just as you say after childbirth,
"Never again."

CAN ID

"Nationalism is every country's bane."

— Vita Glass

ID

We are what we eat. We are what we do. We are what we say. We are what we think. We are what we hope for. We are what we fear. We are what we seek. We are what we hide. We are what we hate. We are what we love. We are what we want. We are what we scorn. We are what we destroy. We are what we nurture. We are what we lose. We are what we achieve. We are what we mock. We are what we laud. We are what we loath. We are what we worship. We are what we sculpt. We are what we paint. We are what we write. We are what we believe. We are not what we believe. We are what we know. We are not what we know. We know not what we are. We are that we are.

❖

IMAGINE

There is a global party. You are invited. A large brightly lit hall is abuzz with voices from every corner of the world. Someone takes your coat and asks your nationality. You are conducted past the hall to room whose door bears the name of your country engraved on a brass plate. This is where you will spend your evening.

❖

CAN ID

I want a Canadian identity. I want a Mohawk identity. I want a Quebècois identity. I want a Punjabi identity. I want an Anglo identity. I want a Francophone identity. I want an Anglo-Saxon identity. I want a Franglo-saxaphone identity. I want a Mètis identity, a Celtic identity, a North American identity, a West African identity. I want a Rural identity, an Urban identity, an East Indian identity. I want a Black identity. I want a White identity. I want a Ukranian identity. I want a Kwakiutl identity. I want a Father-of-Six, a Youngest-of-Eleven identity. I want an Acadian identity. I want a Gay identity. I want a Straight identity. I want Smouldering Red-hot identity. I want a Cuban identity, an Asian identity. I want a Guerilla Grrrl identity, a Staid Old Male identity. I want an Inuit identity, a Scottish-Presbyterian identity. I want an Ex-stripper-reformed-addict identity. I want a Prairie identity. I want a Devout Catholic identity. I want a Twenty-first Century identity, a Pan-Pacific identity, a Jewish identity, a Muslim identity, a Great Northern identity. I want a Long-and-Troubled identity. I want a Maritime identity. I want a Maple Leafs identity. I want an Oilers identity. I want a Seventh-generation identity, a Single Mother identity. I want a Recent Immigrant identity. I want a Baby-boomlet identity, a Hindu identity, a Minimalist identity. I want a flamboyant Flamenco-dancing identity. In a rubber dress. I want a Japanese identity. I want a Post-modern identity. I want a frost-bitten Mountain-climbing identity, a Rugged Old

Logger identity, a Ragged Old Hippie identity. I want a Hip identity, a Cool identity, a Green identity. I want a Purple identity. I want a Gen-X identity. I want a Genetically-modified identity. I want a Kentucky Fried identity. I want a T-shirt.

❖

A CANADIAN'S PRAYER

From strong brown forearms kneading warm fragrant dough in geranium-scented cat-infested kitchens, Lord deliver us.

From cigarettes held to trembling flames in cupped hands under concrete viaducts on rain-swept nights in the city, Lord deliver us.

From journeys in landscapes of loss and desire, Lord deliver us.

From laconic Maritimers with Atlantic blue eyes, Lord deliver us.

From all confessional accounts of rude sexual awakenings, Lord deliver us and deliver us also from any gritty tale of an edgy encounter in a grimy bar.

From the ageless winds of the earth and the possibility of communion with a dank old Douglas Fir, Lord deliver us.

From a visit to Saskatchewan in the thirties — or forties, or fifties — Lord deliver us.

Or Manitoba, Lord.

And from every peril of the printed page, the breathy present tense, the lovers lying like spoons in a drawer, the eyes flicking restlessly, the feet crunching over gravel, snow, the men and women who stand looking out of doorways, and especially, Lord, from the words, "That summer . . . " deliver us now and forever. Amen.

❖

IN THIS COUNTRY

THERE IS FRENCH IMMERSION. Monsieur Hughes and Madame O'Hallorhan teach French to the English-speaking children of parents who believe that better job prospects will be available to their bilingual scions. At recess the children can be heard calling to one another: *Hey, no way, no fair!* Passez la balle to moi, *dickhead!* In this country education is the primary BUILDING BLOCK OF THE ECONOMY.

WE RESPECT THE VOICES OF OUR FIRST NATIONS. At multi-cultural festivals we often give them them a whole stage of their own. We place it off a little to the side so that it can be closer to the forest. We all know how much they love nature.

THERE IS ANOTHER COUNTRY CALLED QUEBEC. Many citizens would like Quebec to declare its independence so that they could go ABROAD for their holidays just like their parents and grandparents in England. They believe the cheese in Quebec would be WAY better.

THERE ARE MEN WHO BUILD THEIR OWN HOUSES OUT OF TREE TRUNKS. Not logs. Whole tree trunks. Whole houses. Three and a half thousand square feet. A hundred and ninety-eight tree trunks. And not log cabins. No. We are talking oak floors, french windows (eleven hundred and fifty-eight dollars), decks, jacuzzis and hot tubs. The men who build them fish for forty-eight pound salmon, hunt for half-tonne moose in their two-tonne four-wheel drive pick-ups. They drive fifteen hundred miles to do that. Good God. These men live in the second largest country in the world.

THE SKIES ARE FILLED WITH POETS. They criss-cross the land scanning for venues. When they find one, they come briefly to earth, squawk into the microphone, smile at the applause and take off again, rising like storks, their legs trailing over the book table.

THERE ARE HUNTERS. They dress in red and black, muting the heavy symbolism of the chessboard colours and their deathly connotations with stains of peanut butter sandwiches. In recent years grizzly bears, accustomed to finishing the leftovers of the kill, have come to associate the sound of gunfire with peanut butter. They have eaten some of the hunters as well as the sandwiches, proving that in this country even among the beasts of the land a sense of justice is deeply rooted.

EVERYTHING IS BIG, it is true. The salmon are barbecued on oil drums sawn in half along their length and the halibut are known to have taken down whole boats. Slugs creeping out of the woods sometimes topple trees that are in their way. Shopping malls are so big that country folk visit them for holidays and queue to take the guided tours. Even the sky in this country is bigger than in others. Immigrants caught suddenly out in the open burrow with their bare hands to escape it. When it snows, people and cars are lost for many months, buildings disappear, and all that remains of the towns is a white moonscape of craters, smoke issuing from each one indicating where the chimneys are. Underneath, the populace is eating Doritos. Hockey is very, very big. And yes, maple leaves. These too are big and float like place mats on the air. This country is the home of the giant cedar. When it falls, the tremors can be felt in Japan.

THERE IS AN IDENTITY CRISIS, a delicate crystal edifice cleverly constructed by academics and media folk who have no trouble at all identifying themselves to each other in smart bars in the city. The artists, working feverishly to solve the crisis in the thin air of the crystal tower, have not yet realized that they too could be in the bar.

THERE ARE BEARS. They are beloved of hikers who carry pepper spray and knives, and wear bells and whistles so that they can safely venuture far enough into the bears' territory to glimpse one, drinking at a stream, possibly, in the manner of *Wild Kingdom*, and hopefully on the other side. The hikers' familiar presence causes the bears to throw caution to the winds and venture reciprocally closer to the hikers' personal space. Reckless bears are routinely netted by wildlife officers and transported by air to remote regions. The hikers then buy maps of these regions and more expensive boots . . .

THERE IS HOCKEY.

THERE ARE SOME THINGS, HOWEVER, THAT MUST BE SAID and this is one of them: there have been other moments in history when large numbers of citizens have watched men hit each other in arenas.

THERE IS TRAFFIC SENSE. Many of the citizens wear white at night when walking on unlit roads. Some of them wear fluorescent vests and battery operated flashers on their shoes. They are most often seen to take these precautions in areas where cars rarely leave their carports after dark unless it is for the driver to go to the corner store to change a movie.

THERE IS HEALTH AND SAFETY: chlorine, air bags, fluoride, bst, edta, mouthwash, vaccines, margarine, radio-active smoke alarms, Roundup-ready wheat and lots and lots of washable vinyl. Everyone is pleased that there is no more urea formaldehyde.

WE CARE FOR EACH OTHER. We may be fired from our jobs if, working at certain stores, we fail to look the citizen in the eye while enunciating 'have a nice day.'

WE ARE READY FOR A DISASTER. Everyone else has had one. Some of our cities have specially prepared buses which stand ready to speed to the scene at a moment's notice with coffee and blankets, juice and granola bars. Ours is the called the Beacon Bus. A lighted beacon in the dark of our dismay. Lit with compassion. Consolation and goodwill on wheels. When a frightened bank-robber holed up in a city apartment block, the evacuated residents were at once able to wrap themselves in blankets and hug each other in front of the bus. Survivors.

❖

THE QUESTION

There was once a town whose name was known throughout the land on account of its inhabitants' ability to live peaceably and well while neighbouring towns on every side were beset with violence and with vice. In the next valley was

Little Filth, that had dirtied its rivers and the very air that hung above it, and Strife, whose inhabitants scarcely slept for fear of being murdered in their beds by the neighbours they provoked. Just to the south, the people of the twin municipalities of Oink and Oink Munster spent every waking minute amassing toppling piles of golden coins while not far off in Skinner's Hole the villagers went about in rags through which their ribs poked pitifully. The city of Bonkers stood a little further off. From time to time, huge explosions within its walls sent clouds of evil smelling gas floating towards the other villages. At night strange, obscene creatures crept from its gates and went abroad to mate with whatever moving thing they could find. Residents of the amalgamated townships of Power and Might roamed at will, it was said, and were never averse to a bout of looting and pillage. I could go on.

But to return to our town — whose name was Middling — let it not be said that the inhabitants were without stain. They had, it is true, a rapacious past for which they made only small gestures of atonement. And there were, to be sure, bullies and thieves and miscreants among them, the greedy and the selfish, too. Still, Fortune had it that over the years the inhabitants had passed a number of almost wise decrees. And so, while their town was not perfect, it was nevertheless a not undesirable place to dwell.

Now, the people of Middling had not only busy hands but busy minds. They loved to gather to discourse on life. They loved to read and write and they spent some portion of their time creating works of art with which to delight one another. It so happened that one day, while a group of clever men and women were amusing themselves with witty discourse and warm scotch during the intermission of a play, one of their number suddenly spoke — out of the blue as it were — and asked, "Who are we?"

His listeners looked at him, bemused. They knew perfectly well who they were. They were the men and women of Middling. Had their friend perhaps sustained a blow to the head? Apparently not. And yet he persisted. He was a clever man and his friends did not want to appear slow. He began to expound at length on on his question, pointing in the direction of the distant towns.

The men and women of those places, he said, may not be happy but at least they know who they are and where they come from. Middling, he said, has nothing to distinguish it. How will we ever know who we are without a distinguishing feature?

One of his listeners at once died laughing. The untimely death was taken as a sign by the rest that respect was to be accorded to the speaker and his question honoured. And so they fell to discussing it.

The evening drew to a close. The men and women heard the muffled sound of applause from within the hall. Their play was over. The second half had begun and finished without them and the curtain had come down. They were still in the bar. No matter, said one of the women. We can resume our discussion tomorrow.

And they did.

Now, because the answer — "We are the men and women of Middling" — was virtually the same as the question — "Who are we, the men and women of Middling?" — it not surprisingly eluded them. For many years all their thought and the last ounce of their energy was devoted to the question. Everyone asked it, the craftsmen and women, the tradesmen and women, the labourers, the schoolteacher, the preacher, the rich family on the hill, the councellors, the merchants and the farmers. It mattered to them not a whit that strife and disease were rife throughout the remainder of the land. All that mattered to them was the question.

It was not long before the people (who, you will remember, had busy minds) began to notice that every book they opened contained the same words: "Who are we?" They stopped reading. They stopped going to performances for fear of hearing the same words again and they turned away from paintings for they knew that there, encoded in the fruit and the flowers, the leaves and blades of grass they would find the words, "Who are we?" They longed for the time to come again when they could listen to stories about love and lust, pity, delight, wit, beauty, madness, and grief, generosity, fortitude, hope, hate, courage, sacrifice, loss and desire, fulfilment and death — when they could hear again stories of whom they might become.

In an effort to answer the question, the town council decreed that all thoughts of love and lust, pity, delight, wit, beauty, madness, and grief . . . should be suspended while work on a street of mirrors proceeded. Everyone worked feverishly at the task until it was done and afterwards many days were consumed in staring at the shining planes.

Soon the people forgot all about love and lust, pity and delight . . . They became used to the idea that they did not know who they were. They began to tell stories about it. As the moon rose over the town's roof tops, the childrens' guardians put them to sleep with the words: "Once upon a time, there lived a young girl and a young boy who did not know who they were so they set out across the land to find out." Every story unfolded the same way. Every story ended the same way. No matter what the variations, the young boy and the young girl would finish by going to the street of mirrors to gaze upon themselves.

Some of the people grew restless hearing the same thing day after day and began to resist. They gathered together to tell the old stories of love, of lust . . . But the words did not come easily and they fell instead to ammending old by-laws. It became the thing they loved to do and they looked forward each week to their meetings. Soon, there were no more by-laws to approve or ammend. It was time for a mission statement! One that would hold for every man, woman and child in the town. They would have copies printed in the approved colours. Then one of the clever folk cried, "Wait! Before we can decide our goals we must ask ourselves who we are."

There was something of a silence while each one privately entertained a sense of déjà vu. And though they talked and talked until their hair faded and fell from their heads and their teeth rotted and dropped into the pale webs about their feet, still they could not move themselves from the question, and were indeed still deeply engaged in earnest debate when a poor man from Skinner's Hole looked down from the hill.

CAUGHT

THERE'S AN INTELLECTUAL GAME that pre-adolescents like to play, an evolved variation of the riddle. I suspect Edward de Bono launched it into the common culture; it involves deducing the set of events that lead to a specified set of circumstances. Here's mine: I'm standing in the middle of my kitchen with a small, hand-held tape recorder pressed to my ear. Behind me, a couple of metres away in the next room, three men are wielding sledgehammers and crow bars. If an asteroid were to hit, say, Vancouver, at this very moment and bury us all in a layer of dust fifty metres deep, I should be happy. Archaeologists thousands of years from now would be hard put to explain the smile on my face.

On a recent visit to my mother's home, the family photographs were once again hauled out for entertainment. She keeps a couple of fat albums but the rest of the photographs, the 'snaps', are stuffed in brown paper bags and manila envelopes. The oldest of them slide around in a large flat lingerie box from the time when there was such a thing as a haberdashery, when shop assistants stood behind a glass counter, and wares were folded in shallow drawers behind them, floor to ceiling. "Show me that one."

The lingerie box holds the choicest, rarest glimpses of the past, black and white Kodaks, squarish in format and with a white border. As a child, I always searched for the same one: a woman with a fur coat and a film star smile. She's at the rail of a ship and she's clutching a fluffy white dog under her arm. The dog is receiving no attention at all. He's just a prop, but probably used to it. Her smile is all for the camera. Every time I saw the picture I willed this woman to be my great aunt Nellie who ran away to Canada when she was eighteen. But it isn't. It's her glamorous friend Lula and I never did get to bask in the beam of those teeth.

The oldest photographs are anybody's, are everybody's. Corseted young women with busts stuffed into cone-shaped bodices of silk and velvet, unsmiling men with buttoned up jackets and vests and hair like polished boot caps; white-haired old men with giant moustaches, extras for *Masterpiece Theatre.* And it is, sadly, theatre. Most of them are studio portraits and so preclude all nosing into their private lives. No one thinks to write on the back of these. We have to ask every time: *Is this a Harrision or a Lane? This was Grandad's brother, right?* I feel I ought to derive rich significance from gazing at these portraits, thrum with the blood of my ancestors, but I don't. There is the odd exception. The great uncle who died in the war has acquired lasting familiarity and lasting vitality through stories told and retold about him. He has accumulated not dust but the mystique of heroism and sacrifice and exerts easy power from his place on the mantelpiece. But in general the significance of personal photographs can be read, felt only — apart from the photographer — by the subject and those who knew the subject alive. An informal photograph of my mother and her sister in the garden, five and two respectively, holding hands side by side in their new velvet dresses and with their hair tied with big ribbons, is one I can look at again and again. I know who held the camera, who made the dresses. I know the personalities these two acquired and I know what their lives hold in store. To others, the photograph is interesting only for its period detail. The significance is all in what can't be seen, in the guessed at thoughts in the mind of the subjects, in their memories and in the unseen futures waiting for them.

This is why our eyes fixate on our own faces in group pictures. We can fill in the blanks. My own equivalent of my mother's photograph is one that shows my sister and I on holiday with our cousin. We are all three mounted on donkeys on the sands. It's the kind of amusing period piece being reproduced now on greeting cards; still, no one but we, the subjects, could derive such rich mirth, able as we are to see what doesn't appear on camera: never mind that we are wearing wrinkly, sand-encrusted, elasticized swim suits, we are actually poised to gallop across the Black Hills of Dakota with the wind in our long (short) black (bobbed) hair. Our steeds are sad-eyed, rough-coated beasts named after early pioneers in the British recording industry — Lonnie, Tommy and Ken. I can smell them now.

Photographs of children sometimes — adults only rarely — have the power to connect to any viewer, regardless of whether a direct relationship exists. Connection occurs when the self is so fully functioning — heart, mind, senses acting as one — so wholly present it fills all the spaces and leaves no room for self-consciousness. The self just is. Candour is the face of innocence. We are born with it —and then we learn to hide it. Of all genres of photography, photo-journalism, working as it does in conditions of extremity, is the most likely to uncover candour, and therefore most likely to produce a photograph capable of connection with the viewer. Its subjects have been violently propelled back in time to their own uncontaminated innocence and their faces have once more become capable of expressing pure joy, pure grief, pure terror. The face of Phan Thi Kim Phuk — the napalmed girl — though she is nine years old is the face of the infant in pain, a raw symbol for humanity. The young fire-fighter ascending the stairs in the World Trade Centre turns his face upward, utterly open, to the terror. His face both bears and bares his soul. Knowingly, he is about to step into the unknown. It is a deeply private shot and at the same time universal. The face of Christ descending into Hell, of Heracles, and, one day, each of us.

A less famous photograph has affected me deeply with all it has to say about the nature of violence and complicity. It shows an overweight, middle-aged man in Germany some time in the late 1930s, or perhaps after the commencement of the second World War. He is in an urban setting: paved road, bricks, rubble. He is running from his persecutors and stumbling. He is wearing only his underclothes. Hollywood violence, like all things Hollywood, is glazed with glamour: the sexy scar, the fetch-ingly placed diagonal cut on the cheek, the handsome jaw thrust painfully back from a blow. When it's associated with the protagonists, it's supposed to elicit awe and admiration. Real violence is stripped bare. It is not about courage or endurance. The fat man running for his life is both obscenely comic and shameful, his disgrace — which really belongs to his persecutors but is transferred to him along with each rock thrown — so deep that we want to turn away. To look at this picture is to feel the impact of the rubble when he stumbles, as we know he must, and his full weight hits the bricks; it's to know the meltdown of the bowels as his pursuers close on him and his fear becomes dread, becomes certain knowledge.

A year or two ago, my son embarked on the twenty-first century equivalent of the Grand Tour and travelled the South East Asia circuit: Thailand, Vietnam, Cambodia and Laos, with time-out in Australia. By the time I saw the photographs of Cambodia they had been shuffled and reshuffled into a kaleidoscope of political and cultural history: a group of twenty-somethings draped on couches, chilling, one or two directing easy obscenities to the photographer, raising a genial middle finger; a cluster of small grinning local boys with a big bicycle in a garbage-filled alleyway making a peace sign for the camera. There is a large lizard on the floor of a house, its skin a pattern of red dots bossed with white, a grasshopper sideways in its mouth. There is a small temple behind waving palms, the lines of its roof exotic and lovely. And more: flimsy bamboo houses shoulder to shoulder along a river bank, a flat bottomed boat, a street in Phnom Penh, Khmer friends mugging for the camera, a display of human skulls (how to look at this? How?) in the shape of the map of Cambodia. Here is a bay of paradisiac beauty. Here is a tourist friend in a baseball cap, the regulations of the Khmer Rouge prison, Toul Sleng, displayed on a cement wall behind him. Here are lovers in close up, a hammock on a verandah, towels drying. Here, in a courtyard, is the tree where children were beaten. In a photograph of a photograph preserved in the museum, the face of a young Khmer prisoner, about the same age as my son, looks back at me; there are more: more rivers, more friends, more lovers, more temples, and skinny, laughing children, girls smiling widely, hands on hips. I return again and again to the photograph of the photograph of prisoners.

There is an unexplored and unexplained phenomenon at large in the world. When it manifests itself, it is as if some invisible force allows us to sense, without looking, when another person is looking at us. It is why you turn at the check-out and catch the next customer staring hard at your neck, why in a restaurant it is almost impossible to comment on other diners without detection. It even works through glass. The best place to check this out is on a public bus. Take a seat by the window and when the bus pulls up at a crowded stop choose someone outside and fasten your gaze on his or her face. How to make contact with strangers. It pleases me to think of a question that has no thoroughly satisfactory answer.

Stranger still is the appearance of the direct gaze in the unbelievably remote medium (many stages removed in medium, time and place) of photography. We think it quaint and naive to fear exposing one's soul to a camera lens. Many of us think the very concept of a soul quaint and naive. My daughters line their walls with photographs of their friends — all beautiful, smiling, all looking directly at the camera. But not at me. There is a sharp line between smiling for the camera (what the girls on the wall and the skinny children in the Phnom Penh street are doing) and looking right at it with conscious — but not self-conscious — intention. The gaze that makes the direct connection is what draws me back to the prisoner.

The original photograph (in the Toul Sleng museum) has been taken square on so that it fills the frame entirely.

It is browned with age and light, cut across by sharp brown creases where it has been folded into four. A young man stands up close to the camera. Behind him a room full of other men are lying, not a space between them, not dead, not asleep. One of them cranes his neck to see what is going on. The young man looks directly into the eye of the camera, my eye. His own eyes register neither fear nor despair, neither resignation nor defiance. He presents himself on the surface of his face. He has nothing to lose. He is about the same age as my son who took the picture of his picture. And did I mention that he is very beautiful, this prisoner? On his chest, he wears a large card with the number 162. The creases on the photograph intersect at his Adam's apple like the cross-hairs on a gun-sight.

I once went to a house where enlarged prints of the two children's annual school photographs were framed and hung on the wall of the staircase, a pair for each year of school. I imagine there must have been twelve or thirteen stairs. There were no gaps, as there would be in my house, for the years when I forgot to send the money in, or lost the pictures.

Lack of organization is an easy explanation for the absence of arrangement and formal order in my household. The real reason is that it upsets me to see messy, dynamic life reduced to stasis. I'd rather see my children askew on the fridge than preserved in frames on the wall (not hung but hanged!) or on top of the piano. It's what you do for the departed, the great uncle who died in the war.

Following family tradition, I keep my photographs in fine disorder. One of my daughters was seventeen before she saw my wedding photos, not because I was ashamed of the mini skirt and wide brimmed hat of my bridal costume, but because I'd mislaid them. And they are still in an envelope — although I know which one — stuffed in a drawer. I have a rough idea of where to lay my hands to pull out any particular decade; particular holidays or events are more challenging. I'm keenly aware that I should be archiving some of this photographic record for my children. Albums are easier to access, but the sense of discovery, of buried treasure, is missing. The selections have already been made. What you get is the curator's — my — construction, my take, which is also true of the stock of photographs from which the curator chooses, should she happen to be the only photographer. Anyone perusing the album will know after the first page what the rest contains. They'll turn pages with increasing speed. It's like being told what to think. And this is why — unless you are a highly skilled curator — an album must never be presented to a guest, only happened upon and entered with spontaneous will.

But the whole matter of the photographic record is chronically unsound. So many of my own family photographs are put-up jobs. Fakes. The shots are meticulously set up to show each child at his or her most flattering, most endearing — and to make it look unstaged. Never mind the guests. They could be choking on pizza but the birthday boys, the birthday girls, are front and centre. There are all too many birthdays and holidays in our family record. If I could do it all again I'd choose more messy breakfasts, more walks to the bus stop; I'd photograph my progeny putting on boots, bored in the doctor's office, sleeping. I'd photograph them crying. It was only when I stopped photographing my children as trophies that I began to enjoy photography as a creative pursuit. I began photographing their socks (material always close at hand) instead and produced a portfolio. It won a prize.

Photography 'for the record' was never enjoyment and, though I've given the impression I was at it all the time, in reality I did as little as possible. I could not bear the piece of black plastic in front of my face, between me and the real event — life. A movie camera or a camcorder would be even worse. But there's more to it than simple irritation. Maternal love is acute. The loss of a child is lived, imagined with every high fever, every finger reaching towards an electric socket, every late homecoming. What I cannot imagine is possessing a moving image of a child no longer alive.

Some people have photographs from their first marriages. I have one from my first emigration. I am standing on the dockside at Tilbury beside my young husband moments before we embark on a Russian ship bound for Canada. My parents and brother and sister have come to wave good-bye. There are suitcases and boxes at our feet. Our steamer trunks have already been loaded into the hold.

It was several weeks before we saw the trunks again. Many tortuous enquiries later we learned that the freight train shipping them from Montreal to Vancouver had derailed somewhere in the middle of the prairies. I think for the entertainment of my descendants I shall call the place Moose Jaw, or maybe Medicine Hat, though in truth I can't remember the name. In any event, it was a fine thing to live for a while in our new country without our possessions.

At about the same time that we were beginning to feel inconvenienced and anxious, we had word that the trunks had been located. I signed for them at the rail office. Now we looked forward to seeing our things again. We were both at home when the trunks arrived. They were battered certainly and the hasps were broken but there they were in our own apartment. We threw the lid back on the first with the same flourish you might use for an extravagant gift. It took a moment to register what we saw. There, in total disorder, in mighty disarray, lay someone else's stuff. We sifted through. Old books, packages, a few unfamiliar LPs (our records! where were our records?) socks, knitting needles, brown bags of obscure bits of plastic hardware, a couple of wooden darning mushrooms (who were these people? even my grandmother no longer darned socks). There were some photographs in a yellow envelope but I only glanced at them briefly. No one we knew. There was nothing of ours. Somewhere in Canada someone, perhaps a construction worker or a dentist or a farmer, was opening a trunk and looking in heart-sinking dismay at a collection of dried grasses, some early Bob Dylan, *The Complete Works of Geoffrey Chaucer*, bags of clippings from colour supplements, assorted chipped coffee mugs, three odd door handles, wood, black-stained, and a lovely pair of pink suede platform boots that probably got fed to the pigs.

About fifteen years ago, I did something for which there is no word. I de-emigrated. I made the decision to leave Canada and return, along with my husband and our four very young children, to England, the place of my birth. (I hesitate to say I repatriated because of the unwholesome encrustations around the word's root. Patriotism is morphing into the self-righteous pig-headed twin of its hot-headed over-zealous brother nationalism, itself a bane. No surprise that there's a missile named the patriot.) On a summer evening in North Saanich, I stood at our front door, the empty house at my back, and watched a steel shipping container with all our worldly goods inside being hauled off into the sunset. My feeling of liberty verged on elation. I would have been perfectly happy at the moment to not see a single one of our chattels ever again — mementoes, souvenirs, photographs, everything.

The container duly arrived in England (delivery takes about six weeks) and was unloaded. There is a certain excitement in the anticipation of seeing the pieces of one's life again; and then there is a certain disappointment. Think of all the personal freight moving about the world: the cracked tea cups, the unwanted gifts, the discoloured photographs; the knitting needles, the vases.

The England we arrived in was not the place of my birth. The Thatcher regime had worked over the whole country with a coarse grade grit paper leaving an abrasive and roughened the surface on everyone and everything. We did not stay long. Some of our boxes never did get unpacked. Two years later (and I've since learned this is not an uncommon pattern) we re-emigrated.

Now in the course of these moves and several others besides we have packed and unpacked our 'stuff' — including our photographs — many times. Packing and unpacking, storing and sorting, you can lose track of things easily. It doesn't take a train wreck. We haven't moved for a long while now but recently I had to do some sorting and packing prior to having some changes made in the house. The storage cupboards were being demolished to make room for an office. I sorted through what had to be moved, checked the slim pocket of a hold-all that was destined for the Goodwill store. My fingers closed around a small tape recorder that had gone missing fifteen years ago. It didn't work of course, not until I found some fresh batteries. It had been left on it seems while the packing was being done. I rewound and listened, rewound and listened. I was earth tuning into the cosmos: *anyone out there?* There were plenty of noises off: footsteps, a great deal of opening and closing of doors, some rustling and, frustratingly, muffled voices, almost, not quite, out of earshot. And then, back at the beginning of the tape, the sounds came alive, full volume, like hearing restored after swimming. The workmen a few feet away from me had just taken a sledgehammer to the cupboards. Instinctively I pressed my ear to the tape recorder. I didn't think to pause and rewind in a quieter room, so alive, so real, so present were these voices. If I could have climbed inside the recorder I would have. I did not want to miss a second. What I was hearing was real, passing life, passed life come to life; my children's fleeting voices, laughing with delight because they had jumped out and taken their father unawares. Their father's, my husband's, voice genuinely surprised, warm with love for them, laughing too. Another child, who had missed the action, calling out, running for her share of attention. And that's all there was.